Planted By The Water

The Making of a Worship Leader

Chris Falson

THE ORCHARD

Planted By The Water
The Making of a Worship Leader
by Chris Falson

Copyright © 1998 Chris Falson

PRINTED IN THE UNITED STATES OF AMERICA BY
KNI INC. Anaheim, CA
2nd printing November 1998

COVER BY
Tom Clark

TYPESETTING BY
POWERBORN

COPYRIGHT & PUBLISHING ADMINISTRATION
THE ORCHARD
P.O. BOX 80008
San Marino, California USA 91118
Phone or fax (626)403-5780
www.chrisfalson.com

Falson, Christopher, 1958-
   Planted By The Water: The Making of a Worship Leader / Chris
Falson
      p.   cm.
   ISBN 0–9661473–0–8
      1. Religion—United States.   2. Praise and Worship—
United States.   3. Christian Living—United States.
   4. Music   I. Title
    264.2 FAL—dc20   1998
   Library of Congress Catalog Card Number 97-75893

To KF

. . .

Acknowledgements

Special thanks to Malcolm Fletcher for saying, "Of course you could write a book."

Big thanks to Wes Beavis for encouraging and motivating me to not only finish the book but to also get the book published.

To Wes and Eleanor Beavis for gently walking me through the painful editing process and making my notes actually look and feel like a real book!

To Ruth Nelson and Karyn Falson for deciphering my scrawls, typing my notes and tidying my office (now I can't find anything!).

To the many pastors, worship leaders, musicians and singers who have shared their time, experiences and wisdom with me.

And to Karyn, Sam and James for sharing this great life with me.

Contents

Foreword

Chris Falson has the gift of hospitality. Whenever I have the opportunity to introduce him, this quality comes to mind. No, this is not a book of Chris' favorite recipes as the word hospitality would suggest. It is a book about what it takes to be a worship leader and the gift of hospitality is absolutely necessary for the role of worship leading.

There is no such thing as a musical gift that has the power to usher one into the presence of God—only the blood of Jesus can do that. But when someone with the gift of hospitality hosts us in worship, it is easier to relax and open up to the truths of God.

When Chris leads worship, people feel at home and comfortable to receive the grace of God, no matter the extent of their recent failures. It is not surprising that congregations on every continent of the world have embraced Chris' worship songs. They are a direct outflow of a personal worshipper and a reflection of what attracts us to Christ.

This book is not a dry theological study of the ritual of worship. It is an invitation by a person qualified for the ministry to come and learn some key principles that will help you on your journey.

Malcolm duPlessis
Vice President (A&R)
Maranatha! Music

Chapter 1

Why Me Lord ?

"Two roads diverged in the wood,
and I took the one less traveled by,
and that has made all the difference."
Robert Frost

On his way to London to pursue further ministry aspirations, my predecessor threw me the keys to my new office and wished me luck. No last minute advice, no tips for success and no working manual on how to be a music director or worship leader.

Apart from leading the band on Sundays, I really did not know what was required of me. I was naive enough to think that I would have plenty of spare time on my hands.

I was very nervous about filling the shoes of my departing and very successful leader. Although I was a worshipper, I didn't think I could actually lead a congregation in worship. I had been a reliable member of the worship team but I had no ideas on how to build and nurture a team of singers, musicians and sound engineers. I had written and arranged music for clubs and theater shows but that did not mean I knew how to write a good worship song.

Whereas others may have deemed themselves perfect for the job, I did not know where to start. Though a professional musician for many years in the mainstream world of music, I knew I was walking into uncharted territory. My whole being cried out, 'I can't do this!'

I do not know about you but I draw considerable comfort from the fact that most of the great men and women of the Bible were also reluctant leaders. However, they were called by God out of the wilderness and fulfilled assignments that seemed beyond them.

Consider Noah. God recognized him as a righteous man and so confided in him the plan to flood the earth and wipe out all that was evil. In doing so, God gave Noah instructions on how to build a boat that would save him and his family from death. Bible scholars tell us that until this time the earth had never experienced rain as it was covered by a watery mist.

The test for Noah was to build the ark in the sight of all his peers who naturally would have ridiculed and taunted him day and night. What could he have said to convince them of his purpose? Nothing. He merely had to obey and trust God to lead him over the waters and on to dry land.

In a similar manner, Abraham defied the natural laws of age to father two nations. Joseph, sold into slavery, trusted God to turn evil into good and he was elevated from the prison cell to the most powerful seat in Egypt. David, a forgotten shepherd boy, was prepared by God out in the fields to restore Israel as a worshipping nation.

Rahab, Esther, Daniel, Mary, Peter and Paul are all admired today as men and women of faith yet they all felt inadequate and under-qualified for what God had called them to do. Somehow, each trusted God and became history makers in the process.

If you are nervous about taking on a leadership position or lack self-assurance for what you see ahead, you may be just the person to whom God is looking.

In my mind there have always been people with more skill, charisma, experience, maturity and all round qualifications for the position of worship leader than me. So why would God ask me to be a leader? We read the Lord's words to Samuel: "Do not consider his appearance or his height for I have rejected him. The Lord does not look at the things man looks at. Man looks at the outward appearance but the Lord looks at the heart." (1 Samuel 16:7)

The deciding factor for taking the job was my pastor's confidence in me. Pastor Phil Pringle was and still is above all things to me a worshipper. He was known around the world for writing worship songs such as *Fear Not, Binding The Strong Man* and *Let The Wind Blow.* The church already enjoyed a reputation for being one of the leaders of contemporary worship in Australia.

Phil Pringle considered me worthy to become a worship leader. This was enough encouragement for me to take a step of faith and say, 'I'm willing if you are.' I will always be grateful for his leading me in this direction.

From there, I had to follow Noah's steps: obey and trust. Fortunately, God had provided me with a book of instructions to help me along the way. Joshua 1:8 promises that if we meditate on God's law day and night we will find success and prosperity.

Meditating on the words of Jeremiah 17, I discovered that my lack of confidence in myself allowed for confidence and hope in God's ability to move on my behalf. "Blessed is he that trusts in the Lord, whose confidence is in Him. He will be like a tree planted by the water that sends out its roots to the stream. It does not fear when heat comes; its leaves are always green. It has no worries in a year of drought and never fails to bear fruit." (Jeremiah 17:7-8)

The immediate challenge was to be patient and still like the tree planted by the water. During the first month of my tenure, I began each day by speaking this Scripture over my life. Within a few days, I knew it by heart and no matter where I was or what I was doing I'd remind myself that I was just like that tree planted by the water.

One day while praying, it was like coming out of a dark room into sunshine. I realized that I was extremely blessed, unbelievably blessed in fact, for I actually had confidence in the Lord to work through me. My confidence did not have to be, nor was it ever meant to be, in me.

This simple revelation changed my life forever.

Jeremiah 17:5-6 amplifies this by saying: "Cursed is the one who trusts in man. . . he'll be like a bush in the wastelands, he will not see prosperity when it comes."

No longer did I have to consider my lack of experience and knowledge as a detriment to my ministry, but rather as an asset. It became part of the learning process that when I am weak, I am actually very strong, if I let the Lord fill the gap.

To this day, although I have learned many things and increased my storehouse of knowledge and wisdom, the tree by the water scripture is my foundation. It helps me to let go and to let God fill the platform, the church building, the worship team, the congregation, my family, my finances and, in fact, whatever He wants with His presence.

Recently I penned a song based on the verses in Jeremiah:

Let fear and pressure fall
I will not run and hide
I'll be like a tree, planted by the water
I'll put my confidence in the risen Lord
And when the sun is burning

And everything seems dry
I'll be like a tree, planted by the water
I'll put my confidence in the risen Lord

Let drought turn into famine
I will not lose my faith
I'll be like a tree, planted by the water
I'll put my confidence in the risen Lord

And there will be a season
For me to bear my fruit
I'll be like a tree, planted by the water
I'll put my confidence in the risen Lord

My greatest times of success in ministry have been the result of me getting out of God's way. No matter how small the problem, it is always too big for me to handle on my own so I step aside (eventually) and let Him take over. Whether I am leading worship, writing a song, counseling a friend or, like David, facing Goliath in my path, there is a recognition that He is God and I am not; that He will give grace to the humble and lift me up in due time (1 Peter 5:6,7).

Sometimes people will notice another's success in ministry and then strive after the same success in the name of God. This kind of attitude needs to find its demise on the altar before God as it is the Lord who opens doors and closes them according to His will for the person and situation.

I know many of the world's prominent worship leaders to be humble people who have never sought the platform or success that God has given them. Each has untold stories of how God has lead them through many difficult and testing times of failure and disappointment. God knows how to build character but the process can be mighty uncomfortable.

Many years ago, I was producing an album and was ready to submit the finished product when the executive producer came to me wanting to add another song. Adding a song to an already finished album is like adding a room to a house that has already been built. It's not impossible but it is costly as it involves a degree of dismantling the finished product before the addition can take place. Given that we didn't have the time or the budget to make it happen, I convinced the executive producer not to proceed with his idea.

A few days after that conversation and feeling elated about presenting the finished production to the record company, I headed out of town for some vacation time with my family.

While I was away, the executive producer decided to go ahead and add the new song to the album. Not only that, but he decided to re-mix the whole album. Although I understood the right of an executive producer to have the final say, when I found out what had transpired in my absence, I felt betrayed and heartbroken.

Over the next few months everything around me deteriorated. Much in which I had put my faith, seemed to crumble. One day I was praying and asking God why all this was happening to me. I heard a gentle voice say that one day I would look back on this time with fondness. I remember thinking at the time, 'yeah, right!'

True to His word, God used the breaking of my heart as an opportunity to rebuild my heart the way He wanted it to be. It was a successful operation. The turmoil eventually subsided, people forgave each other and I was given a new heart, a new outlook and a new peace that still governs my life. I now understand that God's love for me enabled Him to allow me to be broken so that His rebuilding and remolding could take place. The old self had to die and I had to let God bury him.

It is difficult for all of us not to strive. It runs against our human grain. However, God's gift of peace can help us to relax instead of striving. When we freely lay our gifts at the Lord's feet and wait patiently for Him to move in our lives, He returns those gifts with abundant reward.

God opens doors that no man can shut but He also closes doors that no man can open (Revelation 3:7). Looking back over the years, I can see where He held me back from reaching certain goals just to protect me. I have a habit of rushing ahead of Him and quite possibly, I spend too much time knocking on the wrong doors.

I am often asked by people to help them publish their songs or to break their act into the record industry. One night after a Promise Keepers' event, a young man came up to me to say hello. He told me that his worship band was involved in outreach ministry, but his heart's desire was to have a full-time career in music. He asked me what advice I could give him. My simple answer was that he could do nothing better than to wait upon the Lord and let Him open the doors. He dropped his head and said,

"I knew you were going to say that."

He, like all of us, wanted an easier route. The truth is, God is seated on the throne and if we wait upon Him each day, He will give us a map that shows us how to find the doors He will open for us. If we follow His directions diligently, we will reach the doors just as He opens them.

Sometimes I hear my voice on a tape and cringe. My first response is to want to complain to God (again) and say, "Couldn't you find someone who could sing better?" But each time as I prepare for worship, a sense of expectation takes hold of me and I begin to yearn for that supernatural exchange between God and man. I have yet to find anything more fulfilling than helping others enter into a worshipping relationship with Him.

When we can accept who we are with our few gifts and many shortcomings, we are honoring God the Creator. Instead of looking at others and wishing we had their voice, sense of humor, imagination or even their appearance, we can rejoice with God that He has made us who we are for some mighty purpose.

I am sorry for all those years of looking at others and thinking that when I stood in line for the gifts God must have been rationing. Now, whenever I am tempted to think these negative thoughts, I speak these words into my life: "I praise you because I am fearfully and wonderfully made; your works are wonderful." (Psalm 139:14)

Though the call of God is difficult to measure in terms of how and when it comes, we are born with all the right ingredients which, when submitted to God, are enough to accomplish all that He ever intended for our lives.

Some of us are dreamers; others are more analytical. While some are visionaries, we are lost without the practical minded who can work those visions into being. As the verse states: "Before you were formed in the womb I knew you, before you were born I set you apart." (Jeremiah 1:5)

For many years I wanted to be able to sing like Stevie Ray Vaughn and others whose voices had captivated me. This, in addition to always being surrounded by great singers, led me to never consider myself as a real singer.

Recently however, I have realized that the person in me governs the singer, musician and songwriter and that person has been called and anointed by God to be His servant, to go wherever He directs, to do whatever He asks. This has given me great peace as to my natural talents—trusting that God knows what He's doing even if I don't.

All of our strengths, weaknesses and rocky roads behind us make up who we are today. We should be thankful for who we are and what God is able to do through us.

"Now to Him who is able to do immeasurably more than we ask or imagine, according to His power that is at work within us, to Him be the glory in the church and in Christ Jesus throughout all generations, forever and ever. Amen!" (Ephesians 3:20)

Chapter 2

Lifestyle of Worship

"One thing I ask of the Lord, this is what I seek: that I may dwell in the house of the Lord all the days of my life to gaze upon the beauty of the Lord and to seek Him in His Temple." (Psalm 27:4)

When I gave my heart to the Lord at the age of seventeen, I was already preparing for a career in music. My father was a successful arranger and a jazz musician and I had every intention of following in his footsteps. The church that I attended had provided me with a host of new friends and some solid Bible teaching on how to follow Christ but it also made me feel that I would be sinning if I attempted to live as a secular musician. I was encouraged to seek another vocation or consider the study of religious music in the hope that one day I would rise to the position of choir director. In reality, I felt then that the church was asking me to choose between Christ and music. This puzzled me because I wanted to follow Christ *and* be a musician.

Although I enjoyed singing the worship songs at church, at that time the music that I was writing was not of a religious nature. Through a lack of good pastoring and some bad decisions of my own, I wandered off into the world. For many years and in my own strength, I tried unsuccessfully to reconcile my music and my faith.

It wasn't until nearly eight years later, after a thousand club dates and many tours around Australia and Europe that I met a pastor who saw value in me and my music. Within weeks of meeting Nigel Compton, I began to use my gift to help with various worship projects. I continued to play in clubs for several more years, giving my time freely where possible to his church.

Nigel's faith in me opened my eyes to God's call on my life. I could be a musician and play the style of music that was dear to my heart. Nigel helped me to see that worship had more to do with the inclination of my heart towards God than the adherence to specific musical or religious forms. Worship is honoring God in all that you do. This realization set me on the journey of developing a lifestyle of worship.

From shepherd boy to conquering king, musician to slayer of giants, David maintained a lifestyle of worship. Through his Psalms, we discover God the person, loving Father, protector, healer, redeemer, forgiver, provider, not only gracious and merciful but breathless for a deeper relationship with man. David wrote: "The Lord is my shepherd, I shall not want. He makes me lie down in green pastures, he leads me beside still waters, he restores my soul." (Psalm 23:1,3)

I can vividly imagine the young shepherd boy on a hill, watching over his sheep and singing, "My heart says of you, seek His face, your face Lord I will seek." (Psalm 27:8)

It's the still of night and he's singing his new psalm to the Lord. The picture is perfect. What better place to worship God than under the stars. "I will not enter my house or go to my bed—I will allow no sleep in my eyes, no slumber to my eyelids, till I find a place for the Lord,

a dwelling place for the mighty one of God."
(Psalm 132:3-5)

The pressures of life fall heavily upon us. This is reason enough for us to learn to invest one of our most precious commodities, time, in something of eternal value. Jesus had immense pressures placed upon him from people who needed healing, love, forgiveness and salvation—all of which he alone could give and yet, he often escaped these needy people to be alone with the Father. We read in Luke's gospel: "But Jesus often withdrew to lonely places and prayed." (Luke 5:16)

A lonely place can be a beach, a park, a drive in the car, an early morning stroll or a quiet time in your home. Just as Jesus withdrew from his surroundings, we need to remove ourselves from our important business and focus our attention on Him for a while.

There have been times when I have risen early to pray in the living room only to find one of my sons watching television. I remember my initial reactions of frustration and annoyance of having my plans thwarted. However, looking back, I can see God putting me to the test: 'Just how serious are you in the pursuit of me?' As a result (and with a change of attitude), I have found the garage to be a great place to pray and have since made that one of my quiet places.

I spend a lot of my time traveling so a quiet place can be a hotel room, a walk in a strange city street or even a seat on an airplane. Often I will walk city streets and sense the need to pray for particular things for that city and that has led me into some very deep times of personal prayer and worship.

Sometimes, I find myself given an unexpected day which I can spend in whatever way my heart desires. For instance, when a plane is canceled due to inclement weather, leaving me stranded in a hotel for yet another day. Many times I have made the most of these 'gift' days by using the unexpected time to enjoy the solitude and peaceful presence of God. Through some of these worship times, I have written several good songs. Experience is showing me these are precious and spiritually productive moments.

I am a great believer in allowing aesthetics to help us to focus on the Lord. Creation is such a wonderful advertisement for the Lord that when we are in nature's realm, its beauty and character can touch our lives in a way that people cannot. God has poured so much of Himself into the natural world that surrounds us. To let trees, rivers, mountains, flowers, and stars go unnoticed is like ignoring the Lord.

I constantly seek out quiet places that offer something of nature for me to study. In that still setting, I seem to discover another treasure. Gazing at a leaf with all its shades of green, its shape and veins are enough for me to recognize that God is alive and seated on the throne. Wild oceans demonstrate the power of God. A streak of lightning hints of His glory. Without making a doctrine out of any of these statements, if you go looking, you'll find God at work.

When I lived on the northern beaches of Sydney, I would visit Palm Beach two or three times a month and stroll along the water's edge towards a lighthouse. Whether the day was bright and sunny or cold, wet and windy, just being there (and usually quite alone) helped me to relax and it was never long before I found my heart making contact with the Creator.

I can remember a season when I wanted to learn more about the Holy Spirit and how He moved in my life. Sometimes, the Lord would lead me to a rocky peninsula where the water was very deep and where the waves would crash into the shale rocks with such immense power that the water sprayed thirty feet into the air. It is a place where inexperienced fishermen are swept off the rocks and into the sea, sometimes forever. As I watched the water move, I could sense something of the power of the Holy Spirit and that He deserves my respect and attention.

Other times, I would find myself watching wind surfers trying to navigate the bay on their small crafts. Those who succeeded were the ones who could first, find the gusts of wind and then be confident in the maneuvers as the wind came upon them. The wind was at all times in control and could come and go as it pleased.

Keeping the heart open and strong also requires some quality time out. I try to get away for a few days now and then to a farm or forest area to recover from the everyday stress and pressure of life and people. In the winter mornings, I like to build a fire and watch it burn. The flames, in their various shades of blue and red, move around the fireplace as if they are alive and again I discover more of the personality and character of the Holy Spirit.

During the day, I enjoy the long walks into unknown territory to think and pray. Last year I had the opportunity to traverse a field after a big snow fall. As I looked back at the path I had made in this perfect virgin snow, I had an incredible sense of purpose and destiny in God.

My favorite times with the Lord at my home are either early morning or late at night when my sons are asleep. In our previous home, I liked to sit on my balcony with an old nylon string guitar under whatever light the sky afforded me. In our present home, the best times are early morning in the back garden sitting under an orange tree with all the beautiful streams of sunlight filtering through the leaves onto me. Both settings have helped me to relax and to worship Him.

When I worship with a guitar or piano, I don't try to be clever. Inspired by a scripture or purely by a personal need, I will sing simple heart-felt words and try to match that mood with a simple chord progression. Usually this leads me into a song which results in an extended worship time. Often this is where new songs are birthed.

Many times I have sung clumsy words to the Lord over and over again and in doing so a song evolves into a permanent form. Almost every song that I have written has originated from a worship time like this.

I could sing for ten minutes or an hour. If I am patient and committed, the Holy Spirit will commune with me in some fashion—either by speaking to me in a gentle inner voice, surrounding me with peace, stirring up my faith in God, putting a scripture in my mind or by filling me with a new zeal to serve the Lord.

If I get too busy and rushed during the day, then a long walk will help me to relax and prepare my heart for worship. I know that if I am tense, anxious or preoccupied I will not be able to enter this quiet place. As the psalmist states: "Be still before the Lord and wait patiently for Him." (Psalm 37:7)

I remember praying for a young worship leader whose life was full of anxiety and pressure. She asked me to pray for God's peace and anointing to rest upon her. As I prayed for her, a picture came to mind of a dove trying to settle on her head. It kept fluttering above her head looking for a place to land. Though eager to do so, the dove never did rest upon her. The dove, being such a sensitive creature, is so easily put off by even a minor disturbance. It seemed to me that if the young lady could let go of her anxiety and cast her cares upon the Lord, the Holy Spirit would fall easily upon her.

Seeking the Lord does require effort, just as we read in Psalm 63: "O God, you are my God, earnestly I seek you, my soul thirsts for you, my body longs for you in a dry and weary land where there is no water" (Psalm 63:1), and "My soul clings to you. Your right hand upholds me." (Psalm 63:8)

Imagine yourself with these thoughts and emotions towards God. They are truly the thoughts of a worship leader. Leading worship should not be stressful. Instead of carrying the strain of the worship service on your own shoulders, let go and let the Good Shepherd lead His flock wherever He wills, either to the mountain tops or by still waters and pastures green.

Psalm 91 states: "He who dwells in the shelter of the Most High will rest in the shadow of the Almighty. I will say of the Lord, 'He is my refuge and my fortress, my God in whom I trust.'" (Psalm 91:1-2)

With self-discipline and practice, we can learn to seek God and worship Him each day. It takes less than a month to form a habit and that easily develops into a lifestyle. Once we have found the Lord's dwelling place in our life, we can cultivate the same kinship that David enjoyed with the Lord.

In the presence of God is found peace, joy, wisdom, strength, kindness, patience, faithfulness, gentleness, self control and love—all that we will ever need to minister to others.

"The world and all its desires pass away but the man who does the will of God lives forever." (1 John 2:17)

Chapter 3

Heart and Character

"The heart has its reasons which reason
knows nothing of." Pascal

"I have found David son of Jesse, a man after
my own heart; he will do everything
I want him to do." Acts 13:22

The hardest thing to do in life is to carry
and maintain a clean heart. Not a day
passes when our heart is not tested in some
way. From child to adult, the heart is subject to
grief, slander, criticism, hatred, unforgiveness,
mocking and mistrust, and that's all on a good
day!

We know that David didn't live a perfect
life, so for God to honor him with the 'man after

my own heart' title, God must have been refer-
ring to David's openness to change and his ability
to let God extract the poison that threatened to
kill his heart.

Trusting Heart

I don't believe for one minute that when I
committed my life to Jesus I disengaged my
brain. On the contrary, a heart obedient to God
merely trusts beyond being able to understand.

My mind cannot comprehend what hap-
pens when, in moments of deep worship, people
experience God's presence. All I know is that
when I enter into worship, singing certain songs
at certain times, a phenomenon takes place that
transcends my thinking. As Paul writes: "No eye
has seen, no ear has heard, no mind has con-
ceived what God has prepared for those who
love Him, but God has revealed it to us by His
Spirit." (1 Corinthians 2:9-10)

As I worship God on my own, I am conscious of engaging my heart with His heart. I
strum and sing like a child who knows that His

father could never be embarrassed by strange and impassioned cries of thanks. The words might be clumsy and my strumming out of time, but the sentiment and yearning of my heart is what is important to Him.

When I attend other churches or small groups, it is my heart that engages in worship no matter what is happening around me: out of tune guitars, wrong words on the transparencies, babies crying, people talking. These distractions should not prevent me from worshipping. The heart aches to make contact with the Lord and joins with others to make a corporate worship expression to Him.

It is often difficult for highly educated musicians to participate in worship. It would seem that the weight of knowledge gets in the way of the child seeking the Father. The heart of a worshipper must have rulership over the practical mind and this sometimes takes some unlearning.

I had to realize that the experience of worship was more important than the performance of the music. Whereas at first I was frustrated by the lack of skill around me, I began to discover an incredible sense of pleasure in helping others enter into the throne room. I am not against the pursuit of excellence but I would now choose to begin to worship the Lord despite technical problems, imperfections in the sound, an out of tune piano, or a broken guitar string.

Desires of the Heart

During my 'away from the Lord' period, my favorite guitar, a 1974 Fender Telecaster was stolen from the back of my car. I had just finished a club date, it was around 4:00 A.M., I was more than legally drunk and I was waiting to buy some marijuana (for the pain, of course). In that dazed state, I did not notice the thief until it was too late.

I lamented for a long time the loss of that guitar and thought it had gone forever. Two years after that incident I came back to the Lord and shortly after that I heard a message based on Psalm 37:4: "Delight yourself in the Lord and He will give you the desires of your heart."

I remember driving home from Bible college, meditating on the scripture and realizing that God was just as concerned about the little things in my life as the big things. At that moment, I probably should have been more desirous for the lofty gifts of healing, prophecy or miracles, but all I could think about was my long lost guitar. Nevertheless, right then and there I nervously prayed to the Lord saying something like, "Lord, you know that I delight in you, my whole life has changed for the better because of you. . . Is there any chance of getting that old guitar back?"

A few days later a police officer called to ask if I was the owner of an old Fender guitar with serial numbers that sounded very familiar. I checked my records, the numbers matched and within a few weeks I had my wonderfully aged guitar back.

The heart connection is a two way relationship. My prayer and worship is not motivated by what I can get out of God but rather what I can give to Him. Likewise, as I walk and commune with Him somehow there is flow of thought, emotion and energy that satisfies every longing in my heart.

I'm sure the Father got more joy from returning the guitar to me than I did in receiving it. It further reinforced my knowledge of God as a generous God.

Generous Heart

The principle of generosity has helped me to develop as a minister, musician and song-writer.

Not long after the Fender guitar incident and at a time when I was in need of a new amplifier, I tried to sell another guitar. Several weeks of advertisements in local papers generated not one phone call. Inwardly, I was a little relieved as I was unsure about parting with the guitar for which I still had a good degree of affection.

One day while I was in prayer I sensed a strong leading to give the guitar to a friend. The friend God had put in my mind had ten times the musical equipment I possessed and I could see no sense in adding to his collection. I sincerely struggled with God's leading yet I knew that "To obey is better than sacrifice." (1 Samuel 15:22)

No matter how much I tried reasoning with the Lord, the directive in my mind to give away the guitar would not diminish. After a few days of anxiety and a few sleepless nights, I finally called my friend and informed him that

I was awarding him ownership of my guitar. That day was a turning point. It was the day that God commenced the start of a continuing miracle of provision in my life.

Since that day, God has supplied more than I need in the form of instruments and accessories. I have never gone without an instrument or any other form of equipment that I have needed to perform His work. Whatever city or country I travel to, the Lord has supplied my needs and the desires of my heart.

I have been prompted by God on many more occasions since to give away guitars, amplifiers and accessories. I now realize that the tools God has supplied for my ministry are simply mine to use, not necessarily to keep. For as the verse reminds us: "Where your treasure is your heart will follow." (Matthew 6:21)

Although I may have struggled at first, 'Oh Lord, you don't mean this guitar. . , ' with each gift it has become easier to give.

There is an old adage that if God can get it *through* you, He will give it *to* you. This of course applies to both spiritual and natural gifts.

My relationship with the Lord is founded on generosity. He gave His life to me first. I don't feel pressured to worship or write songs to Him.

It is what I desire to do. I am realizing that the Lord takes pleasure in this attitude.

I always encourage musicians to be givers. If your church lacks quality instruments and sound equipment, be sure that there is a church somewhere in greater need.

Between 1987 and 1992, the music department of which I was the leader gave thousands of dollars of equipment to various churches all over the world. Sometimes we would take up cash offerings from amongst ourselves or put on a benefit concert to raise money for a church in Russia or Poland.

Apart from being a blessing to other parts of the body, the results of our giving were evident in the continued abundant supply of instruments and quality people to our worship team.

Broken Heart

The lowest time in David's life was when his lust for another man's wife caused him to commit both adultery and murder. Though David suffered further from the loss of his child, the greatest pain in his heart came from the realization that he had sinned against and grieved the heart of God.

David knew too that God was not wanting an expensive animal or grain offering from him to mend the relationship. During that time of despair, David wrote: "You do not delight in sacrifice or I would bring it, you do not take pleasure in burnt offerings. The sacrifices of God are a broken spirit; a broken and contrite heart, O God you will not despise." (Psalm 51:16-17)

A heart that is inclined towards God repents quickly and is able to receive forgiveness openly. It is a heart that remains always broken unto the Lord.

Brokenness or humility is the one 'must have' ingredient that a worship leader needs to be able to lead others into God's presence. A proud heart is of no use to God. If pride continues to live in a heart, God will find a way of breaking it! "God opposes the proud but gives grace to the humble." (1 Peter 5:5)

I have been guilty of allowing acclaim and praises to dwell in my heart. One particular time was when my songs and albums began to receive international recognition. Without

realizing it, I began to let pride dictate my decision making. It became difficult for me to ask for
help or seek advice from other leaders. A good
friend spoke sternly to me saying, "You and your
church have some of the most refreshing worship music I have ever heard . . . unfortunately
you think you are the best and that will be the
end of you." As soon as he said this, I was cut to
the heart for I knew he was right.

"Humble yourself, therefore, under God's
mighty hand, that He may lift you up in due
time." (1 Peter 5:6) I believe it was the songwriter, Keith Green, who said that if you think
you're humble, then you're not.

Jesus is our role model of humility. He lowered himself from a position of greatness. He
was the son of God yet he became human even
taking on the very nature of a servant. Can you
even begin to imagine the magnitude of this
lowly transformation?

For the past four years, I have had the
privilege of being a member of the worship
team for the Promise Keepers stadium events. If
there is one thing that I have learned through
this experience, it has been about the making of
a servant's heart.

Musically and culturally, the worship has

often been very foreign to me. I don't have a church background and have had very little experience with the hymnal form of worship. However, to lead these men into worship I have had to learn many of these traditional songs rather than require them to learn my songs. I am thankful for these opportunities that God gives me to humble myself and serve others. In so doing, He has caused my heart to grow bigger and more sensitive to the needs of a large crowd situation.

We have to be humble so that His Spirit can move freely through us. What a shame it would be to have to lead worship in our own strength and ability. No matter how talented or experienced we are, we all fall a very long way from the glory of God.

Forgiving Heart

With brokenness comes the ability to forgive and be forgiven. Sometimes in ministry our hearts will be broken. If that's not hard enough, people will speak against us, abuse our altruism, walk all over us, take us for granted, crush our confidence and "slander our name all over the place"! With all this, it's so hard to act Christ-like in response to such behavior.

Yet to overcome our natural reaction in favor of a Christ-like attitude is the first step to recovering from the heartache and becoming more fruitful in our ministry.

Some time ago, I became embroiled in a very heated argument over money. A record company had enlisted several friends and me to record an album for them. Halfway through the project, however, they decided to reduce the remuneration for our efforts.

It was a very hard situation for me and though it was resolved, it left me carrying a tremendous burden of anger and unforgiveness. Several days after the initial controversy I flew back to Los Angeles from the East Coast, drove home and entered my house still fuming inside. Fortunately, Karyn and the kids were at the local swimming pool cooling off (which is what I needed to do) so I took the window of opportunity to come before the Lord and pray.

I picked up my guitar and sung a prayerful song of help. I still felt wronged in my heart but knew that the unforgiveness I carried was going to eat away at my heart and continue to make me miserable. I remember coming to the point of repentance and asking the Father to forgive me for my attitudes and then asking the Holy Spirit to help me to forgive everybody else.

Within moments of my repentance, there came a wave of the presence of God into my bedroom that lasted for some time. Through that worship experience, I wrote a powerful song on the subject of forgiveness:

> *Holy Spirit, help me to forgive*
> *Holy Spirit, help me to forget*
> *And please remove these splinters*
> *That blind these eyes of mine*
> *Holy Spirit, help me to forgive*
>
> *Holy Spirit, teach me how to love*
> *Holy Spirit, show me how to honor*
> *And please remove this poison*
> *That's in this heart of mine*
> *Holy Spirit, teach me how to love*
>
> *And forgive me, forgive me*
> *For holding on to things passed*
> *And help me to let go*
> *That I may follow you*

© 1997 THE ORCHARD as recorded on *A Tree By The Water*

I often sing this song during concerts. Since everyone has to deal with forgiveness, I am finding this song ministers to every heart, young and old, saved or unsaved. After one particular concert, a lady came and thanked me. Though she had not yet given her heart to the Savior, she admitted to needing to hear that song about forgiving others and letting go of hurt. Possibly she was one step closer.

After another worship night in Virginia, a lady in her early fifties shared with me that since her husband had left her, she had been carrying around an enormous burden of anger and bitterness towards him. This had caused her to become ill and had robbed her of any form of rest.

After this one night of worship, her heart had softened and she was able to forgive him. For the first time in many months, she enjoyed God's perfect peace. Her story, her countenance and her gratitude moved me.

In Psalm 32:1-5 we read: "Blessed is he whose transgressions are forgiven, whose sins are covered. Blessed is the man whose sin the Lord does not count against him and in whose spirit is no deceit. When I kept silent my bones wasted away through my groaning all day long.

For day and night your hand was heavy upon me; my strength was sapped as in the heat of the summer. Then I acknowledged my sin to you and did not cover my iniquity. I said, 'I will confess my transgressions to the Lord' and you forgave the guilt of my sin."

Though sin may entice us to hide from the Lord, faith encourages us to repent and to cry out to the Lord for mercy and help. "O Lord, do not forsake me; be not far from me, O Lord. Come quickly to help me, O Lord my Savior." (Psalm 38: 21-22)

The devil loves to bring accusations against us. If he can make our hearts heavy with condemnation, our ministry potential is weakened. Be quick therefore to deal with sin so the devil will have no foothold.

As Peter reminds us: "Be self controlled and alert. Your enemy, the devil, prowls around like a roaring lion looking for someone to devour. Resist him, standing firm in the faith because you know that your brothers throughout the world are undergoing the same kind of sufferings." (1 Peter 5:8-9)

I have seen unforgiveness destroy some people. It is amazing that the victim holds the key to resolving hurt. Though burdened with pain already, we are commissioned by the Lord to actively forgive our enemy, even love them as ourselves. This is not always easy and can take time and pastoral help to unload years of bitterness.

The worship leader has to be free of such burdens and must be able to "cast all your cares upon the Lord for He cares for you" (1 Peter 5:7).

Immediately prior to or following a time of ministry our hearts are more vulnerable to insult. There have been times, when after giving my all, I have been crushed by one negative comment. Although I wish people could be more sensitive and delay their criticisms for another time, it is in reality, our job to let go, cast it away, forgive, ask God to help us, and get on with the job at hand.

If there is a frame of mind that we need to be able to step into, it is that of a peace maker. As we lead worship, we should be bringing a powerful message from the shepherd to his people: "Come to me, weary and burdened, and I will give you rest. Take my yoke upon you and learn from me, for I am gentle and humble in heart and you will find rest for your souls. For my yoke is easy and my burden is light." (Matthew 11:28-30)

May God find in all our hearts that desire to be just like Him. I would love to hear the Lord say of me that I was a man after His own heart. I'll keep at it!

Chapter 4

The Pastor and the Worship Leader

"Reprove your friends in secret, praise them openly." Publius Syrus

The true worship leader of the local church is the senior minister or pastor. The responsibility for the depth and style of the worship falls on these shoulders. If the pastor is a worshipper and demonstrates an open lifestyle of worship, then the church will follow suit and be a worshipping church.

The role we commonly refer to as the worship leader is a position of authority, given to someone who has earned the confidence and respect of the pastor. He or she serves under that authority on a day to day basis to lead and nurture the congregation in all things pertaining to worship.

Once appointed to the ministry of worship, the worship leader needs to join with the pastor to form a team for the two 'callings' are meant to function together as one for the good of the body. While the pastor may teach the Word of God, his partner leads the people in worship to God. The relationship between the two needs to be built on trust and deference for each other's lives, time, calling and position.

Building Trust

A year prior to commencing my 'tour of duty' as a worship leader of a church, I had sat in the congregation mulling over a list of changes I would introduce if ever I had the opportunity to lead the music. I felt safe in my musings for the existing leader was quite settled in his position and I had no real desire to be on staff at a church. Basically, I was happy to play guitar or bass every other Sunday.

Ironically, when I did accept the job a year later, I felt directed from the Lord to make no changes for at least six months. God impressed upon me that my immediate plan should be to devote myself to the requests of my pastor.

Although a lover of many forms of art and music, my pastor was at that time unsure about the validity of some styles of contemporary music in worship. This was partly due to the general attitude of the musicians who had a tendency to impose their views, for example, tearing into some 'bebop' when silence would have served the moment better. There was a tension between the pastor and the music team which I knew needed to be resolved.

One of the first Sundays I led, I mistakenly added to the tension. Our custom at the end of each worship song, was to keep repeating the last two bars so that the atmosphere of worship could linger. This would lead into either the next song or a wonderful time of free worship and prayer.

This particular morning, our musical turn around developed into somewhat of an anthem which, to our musician's ears, sounded like an appropriate musical offering unto the Lord. In our minds, it was one of the greatest expres-

sions of worship in which we had ever participated. The Pastor, on the other hand, felt that an
atmosphere of worship had been broken by our
extreme lack of sensitivity and wisdom.

As I remember, the music in its form was
not improper; in fact, it was quite similar to the
style of worship that the church developed several years later. However, in hindsight, we were
trying to force a door that the Lord had not yet
opened for us.

I realized then that if I was ever going to
introduce a truly current sounding worship
service to the church, the musicians and myself
would have to first earn our pastor's confidence
and respect.

At that time, we only had one morning
service commencing at 9:30 A.M. Though the
best part of a week's preparation would go into
the Sunday service, the pastor would often
arrive at about 9:10 A.M with some changes in
mind. (Sound familiar?)

He may have asked for the piano to be
moved across the stage, suggest the addition of
a few more singers, announce that he was
going to teach a new song he had just written,
or on noticing a particular musician in the service, suggest a special music item. This could

easily have soured my attitude had it not been for the fact that I had made a decision to serve him and his vision for the church.

Sometimes, these last minute changes would require a miracle to fulfill in the time available. The sound board would need to be repatched adding extra cables and micro-phones (if we had them). Everybody would drop what they were doing in order to change the set up of the stage. I would write a quick chart for the new song, rehearse it with the musicians and singers, have someone scribble an overhead for the slide projector and try to keep everybody calm and focused on why we were all there. It wasn't easy and some days, I had the extra burden of dealing with my attitude.

All in all, it was God's way of teaching me what it was to be a servant. It was all part of the great learning experience of ministry.

Though I'm sure there were days when my pastor was putting me to the test, it was not long before he was asking my opinion on how to improve the music and worship. At first I would play him recordings of various styles of music that I liked and would offer suggestions where in the service some of it might work.

I fondly remember sitting with him, drinking coffee in his lounge room discussing music and God's anointing. Our thinking on this subject did not always agree but as iron sharpens iron, we both grew as people and ministers.

We soon began to investigate and experiment together the different ways of making our worship sound and feel like it was refreshingly new. Over the next few years, our style of music evolved into something we were truly honored to say was our own style.

Many of my own desires for musical expression were cultivated in this setting and I owe much of what I do today to that shared time of cultivation with my pastor.

Mentor

I will be forever grateful to the various pastors and elders of the church for the amount of quality time spent with this young and impetuous music and worship leader. I am sure there were occasions when my appearance at their front doors caused them heartburn but they never made me feel burdensome.

I was very eager to learn about the things of God, especially His anointing and they were always willing to sit down and answer my questions. I was quite opinionated (still am) about music and culture. I lacked diplomacy, tact and manners (still do) and so I behaved, at times, in a clumsy, somewhat disrespectful way towards some of them. I was often late to meetings, very disorganized and a little unorthodox with my humor.

But despite all of these blemishes, I enjoyed countless meals at their homes, I was invited to pray with them, and on my days off spent a great deal of time with one or more of them either playing golf or relaxing at the beach. I was made to feel an important member of the ministry team and as a result, developed very quickly into ministry leadership within the church.

During the years I worked with Pastor Phil Pringle, he would often take a few musicians including me away with him on his ministry journeys where we would either lead worship for him or help to pray for people at the end of the services. I probably had more quality conversations with Pastor Phil on airplanes and in hotels than during church office hours. Getting to know him away from the job helped me to follow him during the times when our relationship was stretched.

Moses' relationship with Joshua, Paul's relationship with Timothy and Jesus' relationship with his disciples are excellent Biblical models of how a mentor, over time, was able to impart the anointing and authority God had entrusted to him and to others.

Leaders must make the effort to establish strong healthy relationships with their apprentices. Joshua, Timothy, and Jesus' disciples were products of non-threatened leaders. They were given opportunities to learn from the best and made the most of the situation.

Whereas others could not stand the pressures of servanthood, these trusted allies inherited many of their mentor's character traits and were able to persevere and be rewarded with very successful ministries of their own.

Authority

As the pastor carries the responsibility of shepherding the flock and is recognized by the people as one with authority to govern, the worship leader's position must also be recognized by the people as a position of authority.

In Deuteronomy, we read: "Now Joshua son of Nun was filled with the spirit of wisdom because Moses had laid his hands on him. So the Israelites listened to him and did what the Lord commanded Moses." (Deut. 34:9) Following Moses' example, I would encourage pastors to lay hands upon and pray over their choice of worship leader before the whole church. This public ceremony or appointment leaves no doubt in the minds of the congregation as to who is the leader of worship. Likewise, it helps the worship leader to minister into the hearts of the people.

The office of music and worship is primarily one of ministry and should be considered as such by both the pastor and the congregation. As the pastor prays and speaks faith and blessing over the new leader, the seeds for a healthy worship team are planted.

It is my experience that where there is no officially appointed leader, musicians and singers have great difficulty working together as a team and as a result, critical and rebellious attitudes may be carried into church services.

Imagine a football team with no appointed quarterback. Everybody would want to be quarterback and no one would want to play guard or tackle. I would not want to be part of this team—if indeed you could call it a team.

Timothy's teaching was adhered to by the church at Ephesus because they recognized that he was under the Apostle Paul's authority. The disciples were able to cast out demons because they worked and spoke in the name of Jesus. Remember that the sons of Sceva tried to cast out demons on their own authority but were rebuffed as the demons cried out: "Jesus we know, Paul we know, but who are you?" (Acts 19:15)

The Sunday I took charge of the music, Pastor Phil Pringle prayed for me and lifted me up before the whole congregation telling them that I was his choice as the new leader of worship. This helped me to connect with the church members, many of whom would not have known who I was if the pastor had not notified them in this way.

It is vital that the worship leader be able to address problems with the benefit of the pastor's authority. Sometimes decisions have to be made on the spot.

Some time ago, I offered to help out a church in Los Angeles until the eldership appointed a permanent worship leader. The pastor very wisely informed the church and the music team of his decision to have me come in as an advisor and with that statement, I was able to work under his authority.

One day, during a sound check rehearsal, I noticed some apprehension from the singers and musicians. They were hesitant because they were wondering what the pastor would think of a certain worship direction in which I was leading them.

Admittedly, I had not engaged in a discussion with the pastor over this particular issue but I had the confidence of knowing two things. First, the pastor and I had established a relationship which enabled me to understand his desires for the direction of the church's worship. Second, he had entrusted me with his authority to lead.

Without the benefit of these two factors, I certainly would have had reason to be apprehensive myself. Fortunately the pastor had given me all that I needed to lead the team confidently through this new territory. A pastor can save a significant amount of consultation time by appointing a leader in whom he or she can delegate control.

Choosing the leader is not an easy task. Sometimes you only find out who is 'the chosen one' by trial and error. I have visited many churches where the wrong person is leading and the right person is involved in another ministry within the church. Often the person whom God sends to a pastor as a worship leader does not look or behave nor is educated in the manner that the pastor would recognize.

I remember the first time I led worship at a ministers' conference. It was summer and as the beach was within walking distance from the church, the band and the ministers decided to dress very casually so we could visit the beach. Accordingly, I was barefoot, wearing a tank top and surf shorts.

Visiting the conference was a very well known pastor who was dressed anything but casually and seemed quite perturbed by my appearance. The worship time was wonderful and lasted for nearly an hour.

During the worship however, I could not help but notice the pastor staring at me. I assumed that everything about me, my long hair, my dishevelled look, my bluesy guitar playing and my worship leading offended him. In fact, it turned out to the contrary.

God was speaking to him about choosing a worship leader with a 'heart after God's heart' and that he needed to look past what he could see with his own eyes. He had someone in his congregation with a similar background to mine who he had not even considered as worship leader material. He had been completely missing the direction of God to appoint him.

All the time I thought he was hating the music when, in fact, he was loving it and moreso, being convicted by the Holy Spirit to make some changes in his own church. The pastor and I became good friends and ironically, many years later, he asked me to consider a position in his ministry.

Although I think some people are called to lead, the skills of leadership have to be learned. Pastor Phil Pringle would often talk to me about the difference between song leading and worship leading and this, I have to admit, took a while to understand. With true mentoring, I found myself following his example and though my nature is quite different to his, much of my skill as a worship leader was gained as a direct result of watching him lead.

Sometimes the worship leader has the ability to lead the congregation but is unable to gather musicians. Many times the worship leader is merely a song leader because no authority has been given to lead the people into worship. The senior minister must address these and other problems first by appointing a leader who can work alongside him for the good of the church and then, by spending as much time as is possible nurturing the shepherd boy into a king. The two people must form a team that is based on prayer and a common belief so that the leading of the people in worship is a shared responsibility.

When the pastor and the worship leader are seen to be working together as one, the example to the body will be very powerful. As we read in these verses from Chronicles:

"All the Levites who were musicians, Asaph, Heman, Jeduthin and their sons and relatives stood on the east side of the altar, dressed in fine linen and playing cymbals, harps and lyres. They were accompanied by one hundred and twenty priests sounding trumpets. The trumpeters and singers joined in unison as with one voice to give praise and thanks to the Lord. Accompanied by trumpets, cymbals and other instruments, they raised their voices in praise to the Lord and sang: *He is good, His love endures forever.*

"Then the temple of the Lord was filled with a cloud and the priests could not perform their service because of the cloud, for the glory of the Lord filled the temple." (2 Chronicles 5:12-14)

The question has to be asked: Did the glory fill the temple as a result of beautiful music, extremely loud singing or the simple expression of unified worship? Beautiful music can be found in many places. For extremely loud singing attend an English football game. Truly unified worship is hard to find, but when you find it, there you will find the glory of God.

Chapter 5

A Leader of Leaders

"A leader is best when people barely know that he exists, not so good when people obey and acclaim him, worse when they despise him. Fail to honor people, they fail to honor you. But of a good leader, who talks little, when his work is done, his aim fulfilled, they will say, 'We did this ourselves.'" Lao-Tzu

The greatest model of team leadership we have is Jesus. His ministry lasted only three and a half years and yet Jesus was able to train and equip twelve guys who in turn changed the world. They wrote letters that became part of the New Testament. They preached the gospel to distant nations, leading thousands at a time to the Lord. They built networks of churches, raised people from the dead and unraveled the mysteries of God's law to unbelieving generations. Yet, before they met Jesus they were, at best, a bunch of nobody fishermen, tax collectors and tradesmen.

Preparation for Leadership

Jesus was thirty years old when he began his ministry (Luke 3:23). Thirty years old! Being the son of God, he could have stirred up revival the day he was born. However, his Father had a plan in mind that required time.

Jesus grew up in a regular home in a relatively small town, was trained by his father to follow in the family trade of carpentry, and by all accounts lived and behaved like a regular guy.

There is one story of Jesus (Luke 2:41-52) where as a twelve year old, he stayed in the temple courts for three days discussing the scriptures with the teachers. People marveled at Jesus' wisdom and understanding but no one treated him as, or believed him to be, the son of God.

God wanted Jesus to live a very normal life, to learn how to function as a human being, to experience all the emotions that a man has for his mother, his friends, his nation, his own life. He had to eat, sleep, work, play—all the things that people do.

It was not God's intention for Jesus to be a puppet to jump when God pulled at the strings. His ministry was only going to be of value if the decision to follow the call that would lead to his own terrible death was made by a man. From the very day Jesus was born, his Father was preparing him for ministry.

When Jesus was baptized by his cousin John, the Lord spoke to him, "You are my son whom I love, with you I am well pleased." (Luke 3:22) Up to that point, what had Jesus done that was pleasing to His Father?

Jesus had lowered himself from God to man. Becoming human meant taking on the very limiting form of a body that he had no control over in terms of its growth or appearance and then to live among us as a *nobody*. As Paul wrote of Jesus, "Who being in very nature God, did not consider equality with God something to be grasped." (Philippians 2:6) Jesus' humility is worth emulating.

Jesus waited patiently for thirty years allowing the preparation to take its full effect on his person. His very being knew that God had everything under control and that there was nothing he could do to change or bring forward the day of his ordination. Jesus lived his life, enjoyed all that God was doing in and around him, and left the decision making to the Father.

The Lord's timing is perfect. He may call you today but not ordain you for many years to come. Moses waited forty years. Paul, even after having a vision of Jesus, was not released into his ministry for another fourteen years. David was anointed as a young boy to be the next king but had to wait through many years of wars, persecution, failure, hardship and mourning before he held the crown.

Joseph's years of preparation for leadership included betrayal and imprisonment. Likewise, Daniel was stolen from his family to live and be educated into what we would call today an extremely secular and compromising environment. In God's time, and not until His appointed time, was His plan for the lives of these leaders revealed and fulfilled.

Choosing the Right People

Luke 6:12-16 tells us that after a night of prayer, Jesus chose his twelve disciples. He did not take his cousin John's team of believers, which in some ways may have been the easier thing to do. He handpicked twelve men from the surrounding area (Matthew 4:18-22).

Jesus was not thinking in the short term otherwise he would have found twelve trainee priests and prophets from the local synagogue. He had a long term plan in mind which needed people who were not fixated in the old way of doing things.

The men Jesus selected were not known to be Bible scholars, skilled orators or leaders in the community. In fact, no one else had ever considered them to be leadership material. However, Jesus recognized the potential in each of them and knew that, if given the chance, they would follow his lead, take to heart his teachings and develop into a fine team of leaders themselves.

The Lord Looks for Teachable People

A pastor must have the freedom to choose a team just as a president chooses his cabinet. A Democratic President does not inherit the previous Republican cabinet. He needs people who share his ethos and who will display confidence in his leadership. Having people that pull against his decisions would cause great problems to the government and the welfare of the nation.

There are people recommended to me all the time as singers, songwriters and musicians, many of whom are fine ministers. But when it comes time to make a record or plan an outreach, I choose the people that I know will be with me from the beginning to the end, through thick and thin. It is an awful feeling to have people on the platform next to you who are inwardly mocking the worship or who deep down would like to see you fail so they may inherit the position.

Even though Saul's armor had been a successful piece of weaponry in his battles, it was of no use to David. The armor would not assist David to conquer Goliath (1 Samuel 17: 38-40).

David knew what would work for him and he went with what he knew. Going down to a brook he searched through the rocks and mud until he found five smooth stones that would fit into his sling. David had killed a bear and a lion with similar stones and saw no reason to change a proven method of slaying large beasts.

When going into battle territory, I am more likely to succeed in my quest if I can handpick my musical army. I will always select low maintenance people who, like smooth stones, easily fit the task and therefore, strengthen the effectiveness of the team.

Training Equals Time

Jesus spent the most valuable season of his life training others. He could have gone off and saved the world on his own. He could have spent his time healing many more people. He could have given more wonderful sermons but instead he did something of far greater importance. Jesus included his friends in his life so that they would know what to do when, by his leaving, he would commission them to leadership.

It is a great challenge for leaders today to set aside quality time for others. The boomer generation is guilty of being a 'what's in it for me' generation and our western culture pressures us to be short term thinkers. As a parent, I am realizing that my sons are only with me for a few more years and that they need my time now not just as a father, but also as a mentor. If I can train them to wait on God and to develop ministry gifts in their own life, then they may be voices of hope to their own generation for many years to come.

Joshua was with Moses for forty years. Moses did not keep things secret from his aide, even the presence of God (Exodus 24:13-18).

David's mighty men were from dysfunctional backgrounds. Nevertheless, he put his faith in them and included them in his life. Understandably, they became famous for their battle skills, loyalty and bravery (2 Samuel 23:8-39).

Even when Jesus was meeting Elijah and Moses, he invited Peter, James and John to accompany him. Though it was to be an intimate and supernatural meeting, Jesus allowed the three friends to witness His transfiguration and hear the voice of God. It had a lasting effect (Mark 9:2-5).

During the seven years I spent working for Pastor Phil Pringle at his church in Sydney, I learned so much about being a minister by just being with him. He would have myself and other ministers over to his house many times each month to pray, wait on God and fellowship together. As we traveled to ministry engagements, we would spend many hours chatting on a plane or in a hotel room. Phil, above all people, inspired me to be a God seeker, to be one who waits upon the Lord and one who raises others to fulfill their own potential in God.

The Leader as Servant

Jesus washed the feet of his disciples (John 13:1-5). Can you imagine the son of God, the Lord of hosts, the King of kings washing your feet? Peter was uncomfortable with this situation but Jesus told him that unless he allowed his feet to be washed Peter could not be part of His life.

Jesus was demonstrating true leadership; leadership that is motivated by love and humility. He could have asked the disciples to wash each other's feet or perhaps have chosen a disciple to wash his feet. But Jesus, the holiest of them all chose to wash his friends' feet. Jesus tells us in Luke 22:27 that He came to serve: "But I am among you as one who serves."

The style of Jesus' leadership was one of placing others first at all times. He was not motivated by ambition—to have the biggest meetings, gather the who's who in the crowd, collect the biggest offerings. He wanted every person around him to know that they were important in God's eyes. No one was valued more than another.

Even Paul, the great writer and apostle, continued to suffer as he traveled from church to church to preach the Gospel and train others. He could have easily stayed in Jerusalem and started a Bible college but he knew the greatest witness was to reach out to others on their own territory.

A leader that serves others demonstrates the love of Christ. Jesus gave his life that we may have life and life abundantly (John 10:10). The vision from such a leader naturally includes the welfare of others.

A servant leader helps others to reach their potential and to be a successful person in the community. Lasting ministries are founded on this type of leadership.

Do as I Do

Jesus was a man of prayer. Luke 5:16 tells us that Jesus made a habit of withdrawing to lonely places to pray and seek God. His lifestyle influenced his disciples. When they were asked to wait in Jerusalem for the empowering of the Holy Spirit (Acts 2:1-2), they stayed in one place and prayed.

The good and bad habits of a leader are passed down. A critical leader will nurture critical people. A poverty minded leader will attract poverty minded people. A worshipper will raise up other worshippers.

You Lead by First Going

Often I am asked to come and help churches to develop their worship services. In some instances, the pastor will take me aside and say that the people are ignorant or hard hearted towards worship and that the worship leader has trouble engaging them into a God seeking mode. Usually, the problem lies with the pastor himself for he is the role model to the rest of the church.

Many pastors don't even arrive until after the worship is almost over or if they do, they are noticeably distracted by other people, things in the room or their teaching notes. What signal is that to the congregation? If you want your church to be a worshipping church, then become a worshipper yourself.

In the gospel of John, we see Jesus as a man who enjoyed the company of children and adults of all social backgrounds, attended weddings and funerals, made himself available to others, would happily discuss the scriptures with both religious and non-religious people, reached out to anybody in need, changed his schedule to help others, wept at other's grief and openly demonstrated the power of God wherever he traveled.

The book of Acts reveals to us how Jesus' disciples followed suit: speaking boldly, performing many wonders and miraculous signs, and baptizing new believers. As stated in Acts 4:13, "when they saw the courage of Peter and John and realized that they were unschooled, ordinary men, they were astonished, and they took note that these men had been with Jesus." The disciples had been with Jesus long enough to become like him.

One day, I realized that if I didn't spend more of my time alone with Jesus then I did not really have anything of value to share with others. Not only do I want Jesus in my life, but I also want people to see Jesus in my life. This thought prompted me to write the song *More of Jesus*:

> *The world and its desires*
> *Will quickly fade away*
> *As I lift my eyes from me onto you*
>
> *And though I walk in darkness*
> *Your truth is plain to see*
> *As I lift my eyes from me onto you*

You have honored me
With riches beyond compare
And all I ask of you
Is more of Jesus, more of Jesus
More of Jesus in my life.

The people God gives me to train will become like me whether I like it or not. If I have only one good habit to pass on may it be that of a God seeker.

Joshua learned from Moses to wait upon the Lord. When Moses died, God entrusted Joshua to lead the Israelites into the promised land. Asaph, Heman and Jeduthin, musicians who had been trained by David, were able to bless Solomon's reign. As they worshipped, the glory of the Lord filled the temple (2 Chronicles 5:12-14).

Allowing People to Make Mistakes

When Jesus walked on the water towards the disciples' boat, Peter boldly asked Jesus if he could walk out to him. Jesus encouraged him to walk on the water but, after a few steps, Peter was distracted by the wind and the waves and he began to sink (Matthew 14:22-31). Peter would have never forgotten the incident. I am sure he would have played it over and over in his mind and would have loved another chance to walk over the choppy waters towards Jesus.

Jesus did not remove Peter from the team. It was all part of the learning curve. Peter, with encouragement, would only grow from this experience.

How many mistakes have you made in your Christian walk? Are you still a Christian? Does God still love you? Of course He does. His grace is sufficient for all of us.

The Apostle Paul could tell that Timothy's faith and doctrine were being challenged—perhaps he was wavering a little. Paul encouraged him to "fan into flame" the faith that was in him and to remember that God did not give us a spirit of timidity, but a spirit of power (2 Timothy 1:6-7).

Joshua, daunted by the challenge of succeeding Moses in leading the people into the promised land, was encouraged by God not to be terrified but to be strong and courageous (Joshua 1:1-9). In life, we will all have opportunities to be afraid—it's normal. A leader should encourage not criticize.

When I first began to lead worship, I would say many clumsy things to the congregation. Sometimes people would complain about the volume of the music or my mannerisms on stage. Fortunately, my pastor remembered his early days in ministry and though he would share with me during the week how I could improve my leadership, he always spoke highly of me in public and to the congregation.

Often people are asked to step down from a position without being told why. I can remember a young man who led worship at a church in Sydney. One particular morning, he was having a lot of fun with the congregation but as he glanced over at the pastor, he knew that he had done something wrong. Although he was the full-time worship leader, the pastor organized for others to lead worship for the next roster.

Months dragged by before the worship leader confronted the pastor to ask what he had done wrong. The pastor denied that anything was wrong and said that he was just trying something different. The worship leader recalled the particular Sunday and asked if his flippancy had anything to do with the situation. Only then did the pastor sheepishly admit to his reservations.

For the first time, they began to discuss the issues but, suffice to say, the damage was done. The young man left to pursue ministry elsewhere. Cowardice inhibited the pastor from redeeming a working relationship with his worship leader.

Relationship

Jesus enjoyed the company of regular people and was never ashamed to call them his friends even though religious leaders brazenly criticized him for such behavior (Luke 5:27-38).

Jesus was very open about his relationships with people whether it be with a tax collector (Luke 5:27-28), a centurion (Luke 7:1-10), a widow (Luke 7:11-17), or a woman of ill repute (Luke 7:36-50).

The very first of Jesus' miracles was performed during a week of great fellowship, merriment and feasting at a friend's wedding (John 2:1-11). With the miracle of the wine, we discover Jesus as a man who celebrates both people and life.

I have three churches in mind that have the most extraordinary expression of worship. One is in New Jersey, one is in California and one is in Surrey, England.

The recipe for this wonderful freedom in worship is in the relationships of the pastors and worship leaders. There is no pretense of being friends to the congregation. They sincerely enjoy the company of each other. Their families share meals together most weeks. They plan the services together and most importantly, celebrate in each other's success. In two of these churches, the worship leaders are probably better known around the world than their pastors.

This type of relationship is infectious and quickly gathers others into the fold. Each of these churches have an overabundance of musicians and singers. Why? Because the church is built on relationship. As stated in the movie *Field of Dreams*: "if you build it they will come."

The letters from Paul to Timothy demonstrate a deep love that can only come from many years of friendship. As Paul traveled around the globe he stayed with other leaders building lasting friendships (Acts 16:1-5). I can not imagine either Jesus or Paul demanding the privacy of a hotel suite to avoid contact with people after a meeting.

I find it interesting that after Jesus rose from the dead he didn't rush off to do a press conference to reveal this great miracle to the world. Rather, Jesus searched out his friends to show them that he was alive (Luke 24:36-49).

Chapter 6

Music and Songs

"The man that hath no music in himself, nor
is not moved with concord of sweet sounds,
is fit for treasons, stratagems and spoils."

William Shakespeare: *The Merchant of Venice*

When God created man, He imparted to him both the ability and the desire to create. Just as the Father imagined trees, birds, mountains and rivers before He fashioned them into being, we are able to dream and make up worlds that do not yet exist. Although it could be argued that all our creations are merely discoveries of God's old ideas, He still encourages us to search out the unknown.

Art is a form of expression where man can develop the absurd into reality. There are no boundaries placed on our imagination and whether it be music or song, painting or drama, we must encourage each other to be honest in our expression. A culture deprived of art dies quickly. A culture that encourages the development of art thrives and builds hope for the generations to come.

The Church

The Church has struggled with music and its place in worship for nearly two thousand years. History shows us that when music is allowed to flourish as both an art form and a means to lead people to the Lord, the Church thrives and true revival sweeps the nations. Although we may consider the music of the Salvation Army and the Wesleyan and Lutheran hymns as from another world, they were, in their respective times, very much on the edge of cultural trends.

In contrast, it was during the Patristic period of 95 A.D. through to about 600 A.D. that the church gradually outlawed the use of musical instruments and any songs not written by David and the Psalmists. In fact in 540 A.D., Bishop Gregory rejected all congregational singing claiming it be unholy. The Priest alone was allowed to sing unto the Lord on behalf of the people.

This period of history led the church into the medieval period, otherwise known as the Dark Ages. During the next nine hundred years the church became, on the most part, very small minded and mean spirited getting caught up in political intrigue rather than sharing the good news of Christ.

Musicians and artists fled into the market place to experience artistic freedom. The exodus resulted in the development of many new styles of music and instruments. It was during the 15th and 16th centuries that secular music found its place in society and with it, a cultural explosion that we now call the Renaissance.

There is no reason why the Renaissance could not have been part of church history. During King David's reign, musical instruments were invented to accompany the music being written by the many well paid writers, musicians and singers. It was a time of great freedom and celebration in worship that continued well beyond the reign of Solomon.

An artistic community unconcerned with boundaries or limitations in its expression unto God results in the kind of freedom in worship demonstrated by David who danced before the Lord in his undergarments (2 Samuel 6:14-21). Artists dream outside the lines and then they set about to bring the dream into reality.

Where does the Church stand today in regards to music and culture? Is it able to gather musicians and artists to develop an expression of worship that would make the world stop and listen or is it driving them out into the world where they can freely express themselves unto God?

The Power of Music

There is music in us all. Even the most primitive cultures use music to tell their stories. Music can bring healing, peace and joy; it can motivate, excite and encourage; it can comfort or irritate. It can hint at danger, or war, be mournful or playful. It can cause one to reminisce or cause a face to smile.

Music can carry the emotions of fear, anger, sorrow, despair as well as imitate the natural sounds of wind, rain and animals. It can be celebratory and prophetic. It can bring delight to the hearer and rest to the weary.

When the physicians of the realm had failed to remedy the tormented spirit of King Saul, the gentle music of the shepherd boy David brought peace and healing. The prophet Elijah, after calling for a musician to play, was able to prophesy victory to the nation of Israel.

Richard the Lion Hearted, ill and imprisoned in a foreign land, was restored to health through the singing of his favorite court musician. The French national anthem, *The Marseillaise*, inspired tired and weary troops to overcome their oppressors in the storming of the Tuileries.

Music, in amazing effectiveness, is used in the medium of motion pictures, live theater and televised shows to build atmosphere or add tension to various scenes. Imagine Darth Vader walking into a scene without the double basses and cellos playing his haunting theme. It is the music more than the image that creates fear in the audience.

If you're not convinced, turn the volume off or block your ears the next time you are watching a suspenseful scene in a movie. The result will convince you of the power music has in arousing certain feelings and emotions.

The power of music can be perceived in the way it helps us make associations with certain experiences. For instance, the simple two note melody in the movie *Jaws* that prepared us for a shark attack is now universally accepted as a warning of imminent danger or trouble. The one bar sampled bass line in the sitcom *Seinfeld* is used to announce a simple change of scenery just as the computer-generated music interludes in *Miami Vice* signified adventure.

A great deal of time is spent on choosing music that will enhance a scene on a television show. The wrong piece of music has the power to destroy the meaning of a scene and confuse the audience.

It is with the same thoughtfulness and care that we need to approach a worship service. We must keep in mind the musical atmospheres and the sounds needed to be created so we don't confuse the congregation.

Creating Atmosphere

When people enter a church building, they usually carry with them the troubles of life. Some will have quarreled in the car, most will have financial pressures, others have relationship problems and some will have just crawled out of bed. Rich or poor, young and old each person should be made to feel welcome.

My wife has the gift of hospitality. Karyn takes great pride in making our home a warm environment for visitors. Whether a light snack or a complete meal, the table is always set with a fine cloth, good silverware, brightly colored handmade ceramic cups and saucers, too many condiments, candles at night and flowers by day. The result is people feel very welcome and quickly relax into a time of good conversation.

The worship team needs to understand and move in this gift of hospitality so that the church building becomes a living room in which people make themselves comfortable.

Like a concert by your favorite artist, the sound check should be completed before the people begin arriving. Prior to their arrival, I would suggest you choose a recording of instrumental music to play through the sound system to help people relax just as you would if they were coming to your house for dinner. You want them to feel at ease in your home.

Sometimes, I begin the service several minutes early with a piece of music that prepares the people for worship. It may be similar to the first song so that we can move easily into the first verse or it may contrast the first song so that the change of mood has greater impact. The welcome doesn't have to be quiet but it does have to be warm.

Don't be afraid to develop musical themes for all occasions. Every service will have a direction of its own so it is important to remain open to what God is doing.

Experimenting with songs, chord progressions and rhythms during your own time of worship will help you to be more confident when trying to build the various atmospheres of worship. I probably spend more time rehearsing these themes with musicians than the actual songs for a service.

Breaking the atmosphere is a serious crime of which most church musicians are guilty. The transition or connection between songs is vitally important. There should be a smooth transition between songs so that people can continue to focus their attention on God. When musicians struggle to find the music or the new sounds for the next song, the atmosphere created so carefully during the last song can quickly fade away. Rehearse those transitions. The continual atmosphere of worship is as good as it gets this side of heaven!

The Right Choice of Music

Every melody, chord progression and lyric sends out a message. Our job is to make sure that the messages are consistent. Often the music has one message while the lyrics are trying to say something else.

If our theme is celebration then our music and choice of songs must match. It would be pointless to begin the service with slow songs in minor keys and expect the people to be jumping out of their seats with big smiles on their faces, nor would it be beneficial to have a drum solo during a time of meditation. There is a time for all things under heaven and earth and we must be sensitive to each occasion.

The *Hallelujah Chorus* in Handel's *Messiah* is a great example of triumphant music. It could never be mistaken for anything else. The orchestration used by Handel has helped me to arrange majestic worship services and I must admit to borrowing some of his melodies and dramatic ideas from time to time.

Songs of peace should draw people out of their anxiety into the tranquility of feeling God's presence. David, though a young boy, knew how to soothe Saul's troubled spirit: "Whenever the spirit from God came upon Saul, David would take his harp and play. Then relief would come to Saul; he would feel better and the evil spirit would leave him." (1 Samuel 16:23)

The music should not be melancholic but rather calming or even uplifting in nature. Both music and lyric should be simple, easy to remember and soothing to the ear. Often it will be the choice of instruments and musicians that makes the greatest difference.

Sensitivity to the occasion is what makes the choice of music so important. Sensitivity, however, can't be taught, only caught. That is why waiting on the Lord is essential before each service.

Less is More

Often a soloist singing a song of peace or healing to a congregation is of more value than having everybody sing along. Sometimes people need to be given space during the worship to digest what God is saying to them allowing them to "be still and know that I am God" (Psalm 46:10). It is easier to listen and receive when you are not singing.

Recently, I began a set of eight songs only to continue for nearly sixty minutes on the second song. I started to finish the song after only five minutes but I felt I should continue for a while with music only. I suggested to the people that they wait peacefully while the musicians continued to play. We kept playing through various moods as the Holy Spirit led us. Every single person in that room remained in an attitude of worship and although they weren't singing, there was still a great sense of ministry taking place. As Francis Assisi once said: "Preach the gospel, use words if you have to!"

Whereas words sometimes stumble along the way of truth, music allows the Holy Spirit space and time to unravel our thoughts and minister to us. However, it takes courage for a worship leader not to fill the empty spaces with his or her own deliberations, or even to start another song when God hasn't quite finished with the previous one.

We need to be bringing treasures into each service. Often one of the missing jewels of so called 'contemporary worship' is the freedom to follow the Holy Spirit's leading.

Leading worship is like surfing a wave. Though the rider can decide to cut in and out of the wave, the ocean is in control at all times. An experienced rider will ride the wave with the intention of capturing, be it for a brief moment, its power. Only through years of practice and experience will he or she begin to read the ocean, its tides and currents.

I grew up around the ocean and was taught by my grandfather and father, both experienced lifesavers and body surfers, to respect and fear the ocean. They also taught me how to read the currents and the wave character so I would know when to leave certain waves alone, either due to their inability to carry me to shore or more importantly, the wave's desire to crush my head in the sand.

Several years ago, I was body surfing with

some friends at Southern California's Salt Creek Beach. There was a consistent five foot swell with a mixture of fun body surfing waves and dangerous 'body crunchers.' I remember noticing a set of large waves heading our way and thinking that the first wave would make a perfect ride to shore. But first impressions were deceiving. The closer the wave got, the more I realized it wasn't fit for a horizontal dance to the shoreline. We all chose to let the wave go and wait for another. However, my friend from the Midwest who did not grow up near the ocean, chose otherwise.

Full of enthusiasm, my friend caught the wave thinking that it would whisk him to the shore line. Instead, he was sucked under the wave and dumped face first into the sand. He broke his nose and badly strained his lower back. Being very experienced in many areas of life and a good swimmer, it was his lack of knowledge about the ocean that injured him almost permanently.

If you want to learn how to maneuver freely in the atmospheres of worship call out to the Holy Spirit for help. "As for you, the anointing you received from him remains in you, and you do not need anyone to teach you. But as his anointing teaches you about all things and as that anointing is real, not counterfeit, just as it has taught you, remain in Him." (1 John 2:27)

To further enhance your awareness of the different atmospheres of worship, practice in your own quiet times at home. I spend most of my preparation time asking the Holy Spirit for help and wisdom and even during a concert or worship service I will try to keep my spiritual senses open to what He is doing. I do not want to get dumped into the sand or miss the perfect wave because I am not paying attention.

In the second letter to the Corinthians we read: "Where the Spirit of the Lord is, there is freedom." (2 Corinthians 3:17) Of course, the reverse must also be true that where there is no freedom, the Holy Spirit is absent.

To create freely, freedom must abound. For music to express what God is doing, people must be prepared to take risks and become foolish. As Saul feared man, David feared God. The fear of God should cause us to follow His Spirit's leading.

Songs of joy should be fun to play—with the joy emanating not only from the music and lyrics, but also from the musicians and singers on the platform.

There are certain styles of music that give me joy as soon as I hear a few bars played. I love a good shuffle and a medium blues. Even though it historically denotes bad times, it always gets my feet a tappin'. There is a shortage of good contemporary joyful songs. Some have a good lyric but with a dull melody while others a catchy tune with an inane lyric.

Music should be viewed as an aid to our expression of worship and not the purpose of worship. Both moments of silence and *acappela* congregational singing build depth in our worship. However, the most blessed times of worship are when people of all ages and cultures join with the musicians and singers to sing to the Lord as one voice.

Finding Songs

Before you begin the search for congregational songs, do you know what you are looking for? You don't want just any song. You want a song that has been ear-marked for your congregation by the Lord.

What is God doing in your church right now? Is there a sense of thankfulness, restoration, reverence toward God? Has prayer for the city or nation become a priority of late? Has there been a host of new converts or members this year? What burdens are on the hearts of the pastoral team, and what messages are being planned for the future?

As you wait upon God, can you sense any change in the direction of the worship? Is God teaching you how to be quiet? Are you learning that celebratory praise songs can be as anointed as majestic hymns?

I remember several years ago when a great move of repentance and reverence toward God swept through the body at large. There was a sense of humbleness in our own church that caused us to continually give God all the glory and honor. As a result, I wrote the song *All Honor*.

During the same time, two friends in a neighboring church penned the song *Blessing, Honor*. Both songs are now being sung in churches around the world testifying to that time when the Holy Spirit brought these churches through a time of cleansing.

When a season of organized prayer meetings became a priority in our church, songs that encouraged prayer were found. When we embarked on a concert evangelism program, songs that were of a celebratory and crossover style were sought. When evenings were given over to prayer for the sick, it was important to have songs of faith in God and His power as well as songs of peace and healing.

There may be occasions when a special song is chosen to enhance the theme of the service. However, I have never felt it overly important to have the lyrics of the songs perfectly match that of the pastor's message.

Having said that, I have also learned to accept the responsibility of waiting upon God. This enables me to hear directly from Him as to what He requires of me, the musicians and singers, and what direction the music and songs should take during the service.

Many times the songs chosen have confirmed the message, but it is more important to hear from God than to habitually make the service neat and tidy. If both pastor and worship leader are praying and listening to the same God then the whole service will be a powerful experience for all.

I travel to many churches to share my ideas

about worship. The one theme that I feel very strongly about is waiting upon God.

Although there are several great older songs about waiting, I have found it easier to express my thoughts in some newly written songs. In particular the song, *I Will Wake in the Morning,* expresses a deep desire to seek the dwelling place of God.

> *I will wake in the morning*
> *One purpose in mind*
> *To seek my Savior's dwelling place*
> *I will not rest until I find*
> *A way into His holy place*
>
> *Where the seraphim and cherubim*
> *Lay prostrate at His feet*
> *And there I'll fall to my face*
> *And worship Him*
>
> *And I'll wait upon my Lord*
> *As His glory fills this temple*

© 1997 THE ORCHARD as recorded on *A Tree By The Water*

If it is your job to locate new songs for your congregation, make every effort to find great songs that carry strong, scripturally accurate messages. There are probably more worship songs being written today than in any other time in Church history. The body of Christ is being blessed by songwriters such as Graham Kendrick, Morris Chapman, Denise Graves, Martin Smith, Geoff Bullock, Darlene Zschech, Tommy Walker and others.

There is also, however, a glut of very average songs being recorded on a host of very ordinary worship tapes. A good song is carefully crafted and has a consistent theme throughout. Its melody makes way for the message which strikes a chord with the congregation. A good song doesn't need a clever arrangement; it plays itself. Take the time to choose each song carefully so that your congregation is enriched during their times of worship together.

Writing Songs

I began writing worship songs purely out of my own quiet times with the Lord. A trial would cause me to seek out a scripture. Meditating on that scripture became easier with my guitar on my lap and from there a song would emerge.

The song *Walk by Faith* was written one night after returning from a weekend of concerts. After expenses, I had earned quite a few hundred dollars and was ready to splurge on some needed clothes and a romantic dinner with my wife. Although Karyn would have loved the romantic dinner, she pointed out that the money was needed for some overdue bills.

I had arrived home excited about God's provision but very quickly my joy was robbed by circumstance. I didn't like the way my heart was so easily disappointed so I picked up my guitar and began to apologize to the Lord, thanking Him for all that He was doing in my life. The first words out of my mouth were: "I walk by faith, each step by faith, to live by faith, I put my trust in you." I didn't come home to write a song, but a song did emerge out of a trial.

Other songs like *We Need A King*, *I Delight In The Lord*, *Song From Heaven* and *Come To The Waters* were written as a direct result of what God was doing in my life. In one way or another, God directed my attention to a scripture which inspired a song.

I See the Lord came about after hearing a message from Pastor Mark Saundercock on

Isaiah chapter 6. After the church service, I rushed home with a simple idea and the whole song came to me in just twenty minutes. The funny thing is I did not think the song was that remarkable. I played it a few times at church to mixed responses and for several years, I left the song on the shelf. The fact that it has now become a popular worship song is both a blessing and an amusement to me. What do I know?

Let Me Be A Worshipper, *You Call Us Holy and Righteous*, *All Things* and *Calling Jesus* were written as a result of crying out to God for help or direction.

Standing on the Rock and *We Have a Vision* were written for the movement in Australia called Youth Alive and its stadium events. *One Voice* and *We've Come Here to Praise* were written for another event called March for Jesus. Each of these songs contain messages that are important to the respective movements.

Recently, I have begun to write songs of worship that I would sing to a congregation. Initially, I had meant these to be private psalms unto God using them only during my own quiet times of worship.

However, almost by mistake, I have found these songs to be of great value in the middle of a service, concert or during communion. They allow me to minister to the people in song which then often allows for a more powerful time of corporate worship to follow. Some of these songs are *Pure Joy*, *The First Time*, *Help Me to Forgive* and *Wash My Sins Away*. The irony is that people still want to sing along. These songs encourage an atmosphere which inspires them to do so.

As I travel around the world to minister in various churches, I am discovering an incredible depth and variety in the expression of worship. Each culture has a set of rules and standards, both moral and spiritual by which each generation creates its own powerful style of music and worship.

It is interesting to note that one cultural expression often causes offense to another culture, and yet God will move through both to enjoy a loving relationship in the hearts of all His children.

When writing for your own congregation, be careful to remain within its culture and language. Don't try to be too clever or bring change before it's time and don't be afraid of failure for this can only help you to become a better writer.

All in all, it is important to remember that when teaching a new song, no matter how good you think it is, the congregation will decide on its future. As the old saying goes: the customer is always right!

Chapter 7

Discovering The Musician

"Music resembles poetry; in each are nameless graces no methods teach, and which a masterhand alone can reach."

Alexander Pope

I am often asked to recommend worship leaders and musicians for churches in cities around the world. If I didn't know better, I might believe the myth that the ever increasing demand was causing a supply shortage of musicians and creative people. The truth is, however, that there is an abundance of talented people, for the most part wandering around a spiritual desert looking for a place to pitch their tent.

How do we gather these people into the body of worshippers?

First, we have to truly love them for who they are in God's eyes and second, we have to stop trying to enforce church membership rules that have no Biblical foundation.

Jesus didn't choose his disciples from a man-made criteria. He was led by the Holy Spirit to go out and find certain men, gather them together and train them into a team. Jesus chose men whom the Father had made with loving care and given abundant and various talents. Although these men had been overlooked by other religious leaders, they later confounded the city elders with their Holy Spirit inspired preaching and in one day led thousands of people to the Lord (Acts 2:1-47).

If Jesus were choosing disciples today, what would they look like? Again if he went looking outside the general ranks of leadership in the established church, the people he chose would probably be different than what we would expect. They would quite likely come from the ranks of tattooed gang members, long haired musicians wearing earrings, homemakers, rugged truck drivers, stylishly dressed sales people, and sun drenched surfers.

116

In whatever ministry we are in, we have to let God choose people for us. This means we have to stop looking for the perfect candidate like a King Saul and allow God to show us the unlikely but pure hearted David. Remember, one was a man pleaser and was thought to be head and shoulders above all else. The other was disregarded even by his own father and yet, had a heart that pleased God.

Many musicians don't feel welcome in a church environment. The oftentime strict dress code has done much to alienate people that God has selected to minister through music. If that isn't enough of an obstacle, another barrier is the misguided notion that to be a Christian you have to let go of any desire for a music career or worse still, perform only sacred music.

Returning to the church after years of wandering in the world, I was encouraged by my mentor, Nigel Compton, to enroll in a creative arts Bible college. I intended to finance my studies by continuing my work in the secular music arena. However, as the college year progressed, I felt significant pressure from the lecturers as well as the other students to get a 'real' job. So halfway through the semester, I quit my well paid club job thinking this would please the Lord.

I took a position in sales. I had never worked in sales before but considered my 'commission only' income to be a great opportunity to trust God and acquire a new skill.

For five weeks I toiled, door to door, laden with my bright shiny vacuum cleaners (you think I'm joking?) for very little reward. Gradually, the pressures of not making ends meet at home caused me to be the type of person that only brightened up a room when he left. Concerned about me, Nigel called me into his office. I shared how God was testing my walk and teaching me patience and faith.

Nigel showed me that the distraction of this new job was robbing me of the joy of college and suggested that I try to get my old job back. He was my pastor so I followed his advice even though I had this feeling of wrongdoing. (Should a Bible college student really be making his living from the rock club scene?)

Nigel's pastoring was right. There were still people around me that thought I was making a big mistake and living a double life but fortunately I had a pastor that supported me. On my first night back in the club, I felt God smile at me. It was another lesson learned.

Nigel was a great man of God who exhibited faith in people most pastors totally ignored. His life was cut short by cancer but not before he built a legacy of albums, songs and spiritual children, who now produce albums, direct films, preside over art galleries, principal art colleges and perform in theaters, churches and concert halls around the world. They, as well as myself, are a tribute to Nigel's visionary and Christ-like leadership.

Many church leaders profess to wanting musicians in their churches but they do not make room for them to join. Then again, there are leaders who by their vision not only attract musicians but retain them.

If you ever visit Eagle Rock Christian Assembly in the hills of Los Angeles, you will be blessed by their unique expression of worship. This church boasts more world class musicians and singers actively involved in the worship team than probably all the other churches in the Los Angeles County area combined.

Why do these talented musicians and singers attend the same church? Because the leadership has a genuine vision for music and the arts. As we read in Habakkuk 2:1: "Write the vision down, make it plain and those who see it will run."

The local community is a mixture of Anglo, Latino, Asian and African American, and the music really reflects that cultural blend. The worship leader, Tommy Walker, writes songs with a leaning towards Latin music and Rhythm & Blues that musicians love to play and people love to sing. The whole church is a worshipping church and the congregation, largely because of the worship, continues to grow. Musicians and singers just keep on joining. It is a place where musicians feel free to express themselves and though many of them make their living working for some of the most famous recording artists in the world, their church is where they enjoy creative freedom.

People follow visionary leaders. Martin Luther King had a vision for racial harmony and because of his conviction, he was able to gather people from all walks of life to bring this vision closer to reality.

Coach Bill McCartney had a vision for men from all races and denominations uniting together under the banner of Christ. His vision led to the formation of Promise Keepers. Now stadiums all across America are being filled with men coming together in unity and worship. "Without a vision people perish." (Proverbs 29:18)

For almost seven years, I worked for Pastor Phil Pringle. He had an incredible vision for church planting. It was easy for other creative people and me to gather around him because he recognized our music as something fresh— ideal for the birthing of new churches. We had so many musicians join us during that time that we were often able to send out a whole band of musicians and singers to help to start a new work.

A non-worshipping pastor will never gather great musicians into his fold because he inadvertently treats the worship as a mere preamble to 'warm up the place before God brings the Word through me.'

Worshipping pastors however, have their doors open to creative people and understand that God often moves through the unusual. When the time of worship is given a high priority, musicians will want to be involved. The more their efforts are appreciated, not criticized, the more heart and soul they will give to the pastor and the worship leader.

Even before I started working for Phil

Pringle, I remember that he was a great encourager. Because he was a visionary leader, I was encouraged to carry a vision of my own.

Several years ago God put the seeds of a vision into me that is now growing daily. That vision is to fill stadiums around the world with people who will come from miles away to spend hours at a time worshipping Him. Many unsaved will be drawn to this phenomenon and in that place of worship, they will quite naturally open their hearts to the Lord. No preaching, no famous names, just good musicians and worship leaders who know how to take people deeper into the throne room. The exciting thing is that God has given the same vision to other worship leaders around the world, some of whom are now my close friends.

I am constantly being directed to people that God is carefully preparing for such events. However for these visions to be truly fulfilled, I will need to remain open to the many unusually skilled artisans, businessmen, musicians, singers, sound engineers, lighting technicians and experienced management people whom God will send to stage these events.

It will be a very mixed group of people from many varied backgrounds of life, saved out of many difficult circumstances that only God could gather into a team. My hope is that no matter what job description we carry, we will be of one mind. In this way, we can bring our collective worship to Him and God's glory will fill the stadiums as He filled the temple:

". . .Then the temple of the Lord was filled with a cloud, and the priests could not perform their service because of the cloud, for the glory of the Lord filled the temple of God." (2 Chronicles 5:13b-14)

Musicians in the Marketplace

I travel to many churches where I am told no musicians attend. On almost every occasion, I meet at least one musician who feels very comfortable chatting to me about what he or she does. These musicians, though they may say otherwise, sincerely want to be involved in the worship. However, they are usually afraid to commit themselves into a regimented team where creativity has taken a back seat to religious form.

These people have so much to offer but unless somebody draws them into the fold, they will wander off either to another fellowship or out into the world.

A pastor and several musicians from our church went to another city to start a church. After some time, the musicians all moved on and the pastor was left with his old banjo with which he tried to accompany his wife's worship leading. One day, he phoned me for some advice on how to find some musicians and I suggested he ask at the music stores in his area. He tried this with no response and in desperation, he placed an advertisement in the local classifieds which very simply read: "Musicians wanted, opportunity of a lifetime."

The pastor received quite a few calls and, in fact, was able to lead one musician to the Lord and had two others join his congregation. He drew his inspiration from Jesus' commandment to his disciples to "go into all the world and preach the good news to all creation." (Mark 16:15)

Although I'm sure some may question the ethics of such an advertisement, the Lord moved on the pastor's faith and helped him to build his worship team with professional caliber musicians.

Another pastor I knew was in dire need of a piano player. For months he prayed and though the church grew, still no piano player came forward. One day the Lord spoke to him and said, "Do you have a piano?" The answer of course was "No," to which the Lord replied, "Why don't you get a piano first, then I'll bring you a piano player?"

The pastor acted on this and the very Sunday that he had his new piano, he gave an altar call for a piano player. It happened to be on the Sunday that God had drawn a backslidden musician into the church. He had never been to this church before and wasn't even sure why he was there.

Nevertheless, the same Spirit which drew him, brought him to repentance. Before long, he was playing the piano and has been there ever since. He is now the worship pastor and an elder on the Church board.

My favorite story is about the pastor who, after some earnest prayer, received a word from the Lord for a musician who had fallen out of fellowship and returned to the drug culture. The pastor finally tracked the musician down in an Atlantic City nightclub where he was playing drums and leading a band. The pastor wandered into the club band room only to find the musician snorting a line of cocaine.

The musician was shocked and embarrassed. The pastor wasn't. He introduced himself and when the time was right shared the word the Lord had given to him. The drummer returned to the Lord and eventually became a youth pastor. Several other musicians gave their hearts to the Lord that night and have since become involved in the worship at that pastor's church.

Today that church is filled with a host of experienced musicians, singers, several published poets, a Grammy Award winning songwriter and several very successful recording artists. The growth of the worship team all started with the pastor's willingness to go out to the nightclub to speak to one musician.

Recently I spoke at a worship seminar in a region of the United States referred to as the 'Bible belt'. The church had a congregation of seven thousand people but only had a handful of musicians. The leaders, at a loss as to why this was the case, wanted my thoughts on how they could find musicians. I suggested they consider going outside the church environment to bring in some of the formidable musicians that worked the clubs and studios of that city.

Their response was negative. Apart from having no time because of their busy church schedule, I was reminded that this was not Los Angeles or New York City. Their claim was that there were very few professional musicians living in that city.

God has a sense of humor! At the hotel where I was staying, I had met a musician who was playing in a blues club nearby. We had chatted about music and in the course of conversation, I had asked what the working scene was like for musicians. He told me that musicians were moving there in droves from all over the nation as the city was fast becoming one of the most active live music scenes in America. Later I was to learn that this particular city has more live music venues per capita than any other city in the United States.

After being reprimanded by the pastors, I told them my story and then gave them several other true accounts of pastors reaching out to the lost musicians and bringing them into the house of the Lord. The leadership apologized to me, admitting that they lived in somewhat of a spiritual cocoon and immediately began making plans to go out and meet some musicians.

Ministering in the Marketplace

Once you find musicians and bring them into the life of the church, the next challenge is what you do with them. Do you allow them to develop their art or do you try to save them from themselves and help them find a 'real' job? Some musicians will need to separate themselves from their work scene for a season to solidify their walk and clean up their life. Most, believe it or not, are quite responsible despite the myth, and will develop their faith and strengthen their walk more easily as they continue on in their careers.

I love these words of Frank E. Gaebelein: "There are some after conversion who decide to dedicate their gifts to the Lord . . . playing only religious music. . . with no discretion as to the quality thereof. This may not be a dedication but the burial of God given talent. Inferior art does not become true and good art because it is baptized by religious usage."

The devil does not want the church to house the finest musicians and singers of our day. The result would be that the greatest music of this century would be written and performed for the King of kings each week in churches around the world instead of promoting the 'me' generation out in the marketplace.

As we read in Genesis: "Now the serpent was more crafty than any of the wild animals the Lord God had made. He said to the woman, 'Did God really say. . .you must not eat from any tree in the garden?'" (Genesis 3 :1)

We should not be ignorant to the ways of the enemy. He has attacked the church for centuries with a dogma that proclaims that anything secular is unholy. The truth is: "The earth is the Lord's and all that is within it." (Psalm 24:1)

The church needs to stop dividing art into secular and sacred. Do we have secular or sacred construction companies, plumbing suppliers, film developers, furniture stores?

Why are musicians considered differently than, let's say, the church member who works as an architect? Is the architect falling short of God's purpose by working with regular people in the marketplace to help construct buildings that are not worship centers? Of course not. Why then should people who make their living in the art and media world be required to leave their careers in order to save their souls?

The theologian John Calvin once said:

"The human mind, fallen as it is, and corrupted from its integrity, is yet invested and adorned by God with excellent talents. If we believe that the Spirit of God is the only fountain of truth, we should neither reject nor despise the truth, wherever it shall appear unless we wish to insult the Spirit of God."

If we are fortunate enough to have the first violinist from a symphony orchestra as part of our worship team, this would be a gift from God. Or how about a guitarist from a popular metal band, or the producer of several platinum selling albums, or a Grammy Award winning songwriter, or the leader of a successful rap group? Would they too be welcomed into the family and encouraged (not merely allowed) to continue their careers?

Personally, I want to work with the best artists on this planet. Iron sharpens iron and so for me to improve as a songwriter and musician, I must work with skilled and experienced artists at every opportunity.

How does the church fight back? Could it open its doors to receive the thousands upon thousands of artists God wants to bring into the body?

There are many musicians and performers

who have never heard about Christ and some, in fact, are running from Him. For some of these artists, their call is to lead worship and until they accept this call they will always be miserable no matter how successful their career.

Others, however, are meant to be out in the world providing both salt and light. Some will have opportunities to share their faith through their art with millions, while most others will learn their trade and earn their living alongside non-believers who, apart from Christ, are much the same as themselves. Their purpose for being there in the orchestra pit, the recording studio, the night club or the TV studio, apart from sharing their faith in their own manner and lifestyle is to develop the talents God gave them when they were born. In so doing, they honor the Creator. To smother and deny those talents is dishonoring to the Lord.

Jesus called Peter, a fisherman, who learned how to be a fisher of men. Paul, by trade was a tent maker and God used that natural quality in him to build the Church.

Each musician will have a natural gift that, if nurtured in the presence of God, will find its place of value somewhere in the team. Be also aware of this fact: unlike the inexperienced or

amateur musician, the highly skilled professional musician has already learned to serve for that
is a requirement of the trade.

If you are open, God will give you the wisdom to build a worship team around these fine
craftsmen. There are many He has gifted and
trained for this hour. Know that if you open your
doors to them, many will come and make their
home with you. You will be surprised at what
God is able to do through them for your church
and His Kingdom.

It's time for the Church to welcome the
thousands of artists God has designed and
groomed for ministry in His Kingdom.

Chapter 8

Leading Worship

"He that is greatest among you shall be your servant. . ." (Matthew 23:11)

A worship leader is the voice that calls, "Prepare the way of the Lord, make straight in the wilderness a highway for our God. . ."(Isaiah 40:3)

A worship leader has to be humble yet confident, gentle yet strong, willing to serve yet show the way, able to deal with both compliments and insults, full of faith, love, patience, kindness and goodness—and have a keen sense for adventure.

A worship leader is not an entertainer. A worship leader is a minister. This can often prove to be a difficult transition for people who have worked as a professional singer or musician.

Whereas once they may have mesmerized crowds with their own skill, they now have to take a backward step and allow God's presence to fill the platform. For those with no background in entertainment, the hurdle is learning how to connect with a crowd whether friendly or hostile.

It is not essential for a worship leader to be a skilled musician. A sole reliance on skill and talent hinders the move of the Holy Spirit. Some of the best worship leaders I have seen have been people with no understanding of music theory but whose open heart and willingness to serve made them a wonderful guide for others to follow.

Having said that, a skillful musician who lays his or her gifts at the Lord's feet has the potential to break new ground in worship as well as to gather, nurture and mold other gifted people into a ministry team.

A worship leader needs to treat people with respect at all times. People will mirror the respect willingly. Psalm 23 says that the shepherd leads us to still waters and guides us in paths of righteousness. He does not drag us by the scruff of the neck into his presence. The sheep know the voice of the shepherd and follow his lead.

In every way, we must lead people to God. Some will follow this lead and some will not. Regardless, our job is to lead not force.

The worship leader soon discovers that social and cultural etiquette speaks louder than religious jargon. There are things which are considered rude in one city or country and yet they're quite acceptable in another.

Once, while a friend was leading worship in Malaysia, he offended the congregation by his casual hand movements. A gesture that was merely a nervous click of the fingers was interpreted as a derogatory command to the congregation to get lost. It is important to know the do's and don'ts of each country, city and congregation before taking the platform.

I have made more mistakes and offended more people than I care to remember however, each failure has provided another opportunity to improve and to learn. As the fear of the Lord is the beginning of wisdom, learning from mistakes is part of the journey to becoming wise.

Over the past ten years I have kept a journal of what I have learned in leading people to worship. Even though there are many styles of worship and doctrines throughout the body, the following list of suggestions may serve as a guide in helping you to better serve your local church.

Guidelines for the Leader

● You have the important responsibility of starting the meeting. Prepare yourself and the team in prayer and make sure everybody is ready to lead worship. Keep to the time allotted unless otherwise informed. Do not preach but rather lead people into worship.

● Do not let your feelings dictate the worship. Psalm 57:8 states: "Awake, my soul! Awake, harp and lyre! I will awaken the dawn." If you are tired, wear bright clothing. It will help you to feel more alive. If you are depressed, either change your attitude or hand the meeting over to another. The time of worship is precious and many people need to be lifted out of the mire. A depressed worship leader is the last thing they need.

● Be yourself. Don't copy the style or movements of another worship leader. Use the gifts God gave you. If you feel more comfortable playing an instrument whilst leading worship then do so. Remember, David couldn't wear Saul's armor but instead slew Goliath with his old trusty sling.

● It is more important for you to lead the people in worship than for you to be absorbed by your own meditation with the Lord. Don't close your eyes too much and don't lose sight of the crowd dynamic.

● Be aware of what is happening in the congregation. Do not be afraid to change the tempo, the dynamics, the order of the songs or even repeat a song if this helps the congregation to stay focused on the Lord.

● Be bold. Joshua 1:3 promises: "I will give you every place where you set your foot." Quietness does not mean timidity. When you are quiet, be confidently quiet. The Bible tells us to have full freedom and confidence to enter into the Holy of Holies (Hebrews 10:19) and to enter His gates with thanksgiving and His courts with praise

(Psalm 100:4). When joyful, do this also with boldness. "Let everything that has breath praise the Lord." (Psalm 150:6) Don't be embarrassed to celebrate the Lord in public.

● Without being arrogant, remain confident. If you make a mistake, laugh it off and continue. It is not a show but rather a family gathering. Be gracious and forgiving to others and allow them to be the same to you.

● As a leader, be aware of your example on and off the stage. Don't ever pretend to worship but rather make every effort to worship. It is amazing what can happen when we change our attitudes.

● When introducing songs or leading the people, speak slowly and aim your voice towards the back of the room. The bigger the room, the more demonstrative your actions and leading will need to be.

● Avoid any long breaks between songs. Rehearse with the musicians so that each song moves comfortably into the next.

● Do not be afraid of silence. A nervous worship leader will fill empty spaces with religious jargon. Learn to appreciate quiet moments of worship.

● Make every song count. If the musicians and singers are ready to enter into worship from the first song, the congregation will follow.

● Make the sound of the worship gathering not scattering. If a song is not working then finish it early. Everything has a time and a place. Don't force feed a musical recipe to your people that is not adding to their spiritual meal.

● Never berate a congregation for not worshipping. Be a shepherd. Be gracious. Never speak down to the people. You are there to serve them, they are not there for your benefit. It is the Holy Spirit's job to convict, not yours.

● Choose songs the congregation knows and avoid too many new songs. A general rule would be no more than two new songs per month and in any given service one would be plenty.

● Be sensitive to the age and the culture of the congregation. Make it as comfortable as possible for these good people to worship. This may mean a rethink about both songs and instrumentation. Be flexible and gracious. Remember the saying: "Blessed are the flexible for at times they will be bent out of shape."

● A moment of fun has great purpose when it precedes a song of worship. A praise song with energy and actions can often release people from distractions and inhibitions. However, avoid too much playfulness and too many actions. A sense of fun can both lift and kill a meeting. Timing is everything!

● Don't ever attempt to discipline or quarrel with musicians and singers on stage. As the old Broadway producer once said, "The show must go on." Work with what you have, make the most of the situation and address any people problems after the service—preferably *after* you have calmed down!

● Avoid 'in' jokes or playing up to your friends. Treat the whole congregation with respect, whether they are young, old, wealthy or poor.

They will love and respect you in return.

● Think of yourself as the conductor and the congregation as the choir. Don't entertain the people but rather direct their hearts and expression of worship towards the Almighty God.

● Know when to hand the meeting over to the pastor. He should be able to continue where you leave off, allowing for a steady flow of ministry throughout the service.

More Advice on Leading Worship

Before every worship service or concert, I rehearse by myself the intended order of songs. Although I am a spontaneous kind of guy, good preparation actually allows me more freedom and gives me confidence to let the worship experience be natural.

In preparing a worship set, I will usually include a song or two in the middle specifically about worship. I call this a breathing space.

Some people need a moment to reflect on God while others need help to focus their thoughts on God. I wrote *Let Me Be a Worshipper* for such occasions:

Let me a worshipper round your throne
Bathing in your righteousness
Let me be a servant in your house
So I can wait upon you
Let me hear the voices of angels
As they sing about your holiness
Let me always be in your presence
So I can wait upon you
So I can wait upon you

And through the valleys
Over rocky roads
In the desert
I'll be never alone
And through the fire
And raging waters
In the darkest night
I'll never be alone
Round your throne

Because this song is a prayer, I usually sing it by myself until the very end when I ask people to join me on "round your throne". I follow this song with something that allows us to sing about God's majesty, usually *I See the Lord*.

I avoid reading lyrics or music if I can help it. I like everything to flow smoothly from song to song and will avoid anything that breaks this flow. People will always play or sing a song with more conviction when it is a part of them. The only way to attain this is for your people to spend time with the song, allowing it to become, in a sense, their own. The optimum is that no one in the worship team should rely on music or song sheets.

A congregation needs a varied diet of worship. When a song is served up in the same old predictable arrangement each week, it contributes to the tiredness of worship. In order to keep worship fresh and alive, I like to leave arrangements fairly open ended and I will direct the congregation by either singing or speaking to them during each song.

It is up to the band and singers to follow me as I lead the people. To turn my back on the congregation in order to instruct musicians and singers may be considered poor social etiquette.

A team that works, prays and fellowships together develops an acute sensory perception of where the worship leader will go. Although this all takes time and practice, the benefits to a church are well worth the effort.

Never hesitate to call out to God for help during the worship service. There are times in worship when I become unsure about the direction that I am leading. There are other times when I think I have chosen the right format only to have my confidence sabotaged by what I see and hear around me. While the congregation continues to sing a verse or chorus, I will silently call out to God for guidance. "Because you are my help I sing in the shadow of your wings." (Psalm 63:7)

Sometimes, I hear a quiet voice assuring me to continue on the path I have chosen. Other times, I will sense the need to adjust my plans to an alternate song or mood, from celebration praise to a peaceful song of worship or vice versa.

Remember, Jesus' promise to us: "But the Counselor, the Holy Spirit, whom the Father will send in my name, will teach you all things and remind you of everything I have said to you." (John 14:26)

Leading Requires Faith

Faith is essential to the worship leader. In desiring to lead others to experience God in worship, a leader acts on his or her assurance that God's presence and peace will come to those who seek Him. As we read in Hebrews: "And without faith it is impossible to please God because anyone who comes to Him must believe that he exists and that He rewards those who earnestly seek Him." (Hebrews 11:6)

We have to be confident that God will be present and that we carry His anointing for the occasion. There may be times when we will assume failure by what we sense with our natural minds and yet these can often be the greatest moments of worship and ministry for the congregation. We need to adopt a 'no sweat' ministry. Life becomes simple when we turn up and let God do the rest.

Although chosen and appointed by man, each worship leader is called by God and separated for a specific task. As in the case of King David, God "chose David his servant and took him from the sheep pens; from tending the sheep he brought him to be the shepherd of his people Jacob, of Israel his inheritance. And David shepherded them with integrity of heart and skillful hands." (Psalm 78:70-72)

David's style of leading would be offensive to many religious leaders today. He was neither apologetic nor embarrassed to show deep emotion when calling the people to worship. As David wrote: "Shout for joy to the Lord, all the earth, burst into jubilant song with music; make music to the Lord with the harp, with the harp and the sound of singing, with trumpets and the blast of the ram's horn, shout for joy before the King." (Psalm 98:4-6)

Under the anointing of the Holy Spirit, a prophetic song flowed out from David's being. His expression of worship enabled him to make jubilant noise, dance, lift his hands or weep in the Lord's presence. To suggest otherwise would have been insulting to a man with a passion for God.

It is for each of us to discover through the Word of God, and through prayer and fellowship with other believers, our own unique calling and style of leading worship. No matter how others lead around us, whether they are wonderful singers, charismatic in their movements or skilled on an instrument, we have to be ourselves. When we are ourselves, we'll find God pouring over us an anointing that is special and tailored to our lives.

Every worship leader has strengths and weakness. Some are better at calling people into a joyful time of praise while some are more comfortable when leading others in majestic anthems of worship.

If I have a strength as a worship leader, it is to enable people to experience peace with God. I discovered an anointing of peace through a series of heavy trials and now what was once a weakness has become a strength in my life. I use the song *Peace of God* during times of worship to encourage people to focus on God's peace:

> *Come to me weary and burdened*
> *And I will give you rest*
> *Come on in all who are troubled*
> *And I will give you rest*
> *For my yoke is easy and my burden is light*
> *Enter in*
> *And the peace of God will fall on you*
> *Falling, falling, falling on you*
> *The peace of God is*
> *Falling, falling, falling on you*

Come to me all you brokenhearted
And I will give you strength
And if you cannot make it through another day
I will carry you
For my yoke is easy and my burden is light
Enter in
And the peace of God will fall on you
Falling, falling, falling on you
The peace of God is
Falling, falling, falling on you

© 1997 THE ORCHARD as recorded on *A Tree By The Water*

If you ever need to encourage yourself before you lead worship may I suggest speaking the following scripture over your life. There is no greater mission statement for the worship leader than this:

"The Spirit of the Sovereign Lord is on me, because the Lord has anointed me to preach good news to the poor. He has sent me to bind up the brokenhearted, to proclaim freedom for the captives and release from darkness for the prisoners, to proclaim the year of the Lord's favor and the day of vengeance of our God, to comfort all who mourn, and provide for those who grieve in Zion—bestow on them a crown of beauty instead of ashes, the oil of gladness instead of mourning, and a garment of praise instead of despair. They will be called oaks of righteousness, a planting of the Lord for the display of His splendor." (Isaiah 61:1-3)

Chapter 9

Building a Team

"Instruction does not prevent waste of time or mistakes; and mistakes themselves are often the best teachers." James A. Froude

The team leader does not have to be the most skilled musician or singer, or even a Bible college graduate. Although the study of the tabernacle of David and the Levitical Order are noble enterprises, the knowledge gained will not necessarily make one a better leader of worship.

Leadership is an office held by someone who is called by God to lead and who is willing to serve others and help them to reach their potential in God. A leader has to be a worshipper—one who leads by example.

To build a team, the leader must not be threatened by another's skill, spiritual maturity, potential or experience. The qualities in others are God's gift to the worship leader. It is therefore the worship leader's responsibility to help each team member perform to the best of their ability. A leader does this by communicating the plan and desires for the worship service in a way that is easy for his team to follow.

Charles P. Steinmetz once said: "There are no foolish questions and no man becomes a fool until he has stopped asking questions." If the leader explains the plan, then each team member should be able to provide the answers to these simple questions before each service begins:

1. What is the song list and the order of the service?

2. Do I know the arrangements?

3. Who is leading worship and is the same person leading the band?

4. What is the desired goal of the worship service?

5. What is the length of the worship service?

6. Is there anything special required of me today such as a solo or key change?

7. Am I prepared to participate in this worship service now?

No baseball team ever runs onto the field without a plan. Each player knows where to stand and in each situation, what is expected of him. There should be no difference in the organization of a worship team.

The legendary band, *The Beatles*, is a good example of how a team functions. For less than ten years, the 'Fab Four' shared a collective vision and changed the way music was written and performed around the world. They were by no means the best musicians in the world, but when they performed it was as if they were one.

The worship team is made up of all types of people who share a common goal. When each plays his or her part, the whole can be a wonderful expression of music to God. If there is no order or discipline then the body is not functioning as God intended.

As Paul wrote to the church at Corinth: "But in fact God has arranged the parts in the body, every one of them, just as he wanted them to be. If they were all one part where would the body be? As it is, there are many parts, but one body." (1 Corinthians 12:18-20)

Apart from the actual style and running order of a service, people need to know what is expected of them as individuals. I am always careful not to make too many rules in the hope of building relationships with the team. However, it is important for each person to know what is expected of him or her so that an informed decision about remaining on the team can be made.

The most important requirement for any team player is their willingness to be part of a team. I would rather have a band full of musicians of average talent who share a common vision than a group of gifted individuals with no commitment to the vision.

The following simple and practical requirements for team members usually sort out the wheat from the chaff.

Drummer

1. Keeping time and laying down the groove is your top priority. Every drummer should own a metronome or a drum machine to utilize in personal practice. Keeping time is not an optional extra for the drummer—the entire band relies upon this phenomenon to take place. If you have problems coming back in on the first beat of the bar after a fill then do not fill.

2. Play simple patterns. Don't be too busy or fill at the end of every 4 or 8 bar phrases. Leave space.

3. Listen to the bass player and work with him. The kick drum and bass should play similar, if not exactly the same, rhythmic patterns. Arrange a time for you to practice together.

4. Sing the song as you play. This will help you to phrase with the singers and help you to read the overall dynamic of the song.

5. Follow the worship leader and/or the band leader. Make every effort to be part of the whole

sound. You must be always listening to what is happening around you.

6. Learn to create dynamics. Use brushes, stick across the snare, mallets on cymbals, rim shot, etc., to add color to the music.

7. Don't confuse loud and soft with fast and slow. Practice playing each song as softly as possible without dragging the tempo. Practice playing a song and build the volume as you go being careful not to speed up.

Bass

1. Buy a tuner and use it before each rehearsal and church service. Check the tuning of the piano and tune your instrument accordingly.

2. Build a relationship with the drummer. Work together with his kick drum and hi-hats.

3. Try to not be too busy in your playing but rather enjoy the strength of simplicity. Avoid playing a fill at the end of every phrase.

4. Wherever possible, commit the songs to memory and practice them in every key. Sing along and be aware of the phrasing of the lyrics. This will help you to play with more feeling and dynamic.

5. You must be able to play quietly without losing the sense of timing. Practice this with the drummer.

6. Work with the other instruments (guitar, piano etc.) helping them to understand that too much bottom end makes the music sound mushy. Play in a way that favors other instruments.

7. Listen to the other instruments. If you cannot hear them, be open to the possibility that you are playing too loud.

Piano

1. Take responsibility for the tuning and general care of the piano. Depending on the temperature changes, the piano should be tuned at least

once a month. If it is out of tune or has dropped in pitch, make the rest of the musicians aware of the problem.

2. Be mindful of the fact that your instrument has the potential to override all other harmonic instruments. You will need to listen to the bass and work out with him or her what left hand parts you will play. Also, work with the guitarist and decide who will play full chords or rhythmic patterns. Avoid playing both.

3. Learn each song by heart and then practice each song in every key. This may seem like a lot of work but it will help you to develop more ideas, break some habits and make you more flexible for what may happen in worship.

4. Make each song your own. Sing it in your own quiet time of worship. There will be many times when you will be called upon to play a song on your own during a service.

5. Listen to the instruments and singers at all times. Be conscious of what is happening around you. As with all instruments, be sensitive to your own volume and notation. Sometimes,

the worship does not need you to play anything. Learn to enjoy those moments.

6. When playing quietly, don't slow down and when playing loudly don't speed up or rush your phrasing. Practice with a metronome or drum machine.

7. Avoid filling too many spaces or being too flowery in your accompaniment. Remind yourself that you are part of a whole band.

Electric Guitar

1. Buy a tuner and use it before each rehearsal and church service. Check the tuning of the piano and tune your instrument accordingly.

2. Maintain your equipment. Discard any noisy chords and change batteries in your effects pedals. Avoid at all costs electronic noises during the services. They have a bad habit of occurring during quiet moments of worship.

3. Listen to what the bass player and drummer are doing. If you are to play rhythm, the hi-hats

and kick will give you an idea of what pattern to play. Try to lock in with the rhythm section on each song.

4. Listen to and work with the piano player. You will often double up on both rhythm and harmonic ideas. Work a compromise from song to song.

5. Be aware of your volume. Remember, if you can't hear everybody then perhaps you are too loud. Another factor of great importance is to not confuse quietness with slowing down, loudness with speeding up.

6. When in doubt, don't play. Sometimes the music is fine without you. Learn to appreciate those moments.

7. Memorize each song and be able to play it in any key. Learn to make each song your own and sing along whenever you can. This helps significantly with knowing when and where to play your ideas.

Acoustic Guitar

1. Buy a tuner and use it before each rehearsal and church service. Check the tuning of the piano and tune your instrument accordingly.

2. Learn to get the best sound out of your instrument without using a microphone (which is prone to picking up other instruments around you). My preference is for a bridge pickup into a small pre-amp into a direct box into the system. This enables me to control my tone without hindering the overall sound of the band.

3. Whether strumming or picking, listen to the drummer or percussionist for your rhythmical patter.

4. Avoid over playing but rather make every effort to synchronize with the other rhythm instruments.

5. Memorize each song and practice them in every key. This will help your musicianship and will give you a greater sense of chord structure for other songs.

6. Learn to use the capo and be able to change key quickly. Also, be able to work in open tunings. This will add color to the arrangements.

7. When in doubt, don't play. Sometimes the worship will not need you to play. Learn to enjoy those moments.

Keyboards

1. Be aware of the tuning around you. You may have to adjust to the piano. Carry a tuner and be conversant with the tuning of Midi instruments.

2. When working with a guitar player and/or piano player, discuss each song so you can leave some space for others.

3. Avoid playing too many low end notes unless playing a solo piece. Remember that your left hand in addition to what the bass player is playing can take away the dynamic clarity of the bottom end of the music.

4. Take great care in choosing the sounds for each song. In the quiet songs, find subtle pads that blend with the piano and acoustic guitar. Avoid sounds that clash with, or are too similar to, other instruments on stage. Vary your sounds from song to song.

5. Avoid overplaying. Often a single line is all that is required of you. You will never need to use all ten fingers. Remember that your keyboards, although full of color and atmosphere, can easily overwhelm the other instruments.

6. Again, as with other instrumentalists, memorize each song and practice it in every key. You will be called upon to be the solo accompaniment at times and key changes may be required.

7. When in doubt, don't play. There will be times when the worship doesn't need you to add your sounds. Learn to appreciate those moments and enjoy the worship.

Brass

1. Learn how to keep your instrument in tune. Be aware that temperature alters all acoustic instruments and it is imperative that you play in tune with the rest of the band.

2. Whether a solo instrument or a section, it is important to have some form of arrangement. I would encourage the writing of set parts for each song. Remember that a brass instrument is one of power and should not be overused.

3. Be aware of your volume. Work as a section, trying to blend as if you are all one instrument.

4. Practice playing quietly. Tuning can often be a problem in quiet moments.

5. Unison is often more powerful than harmony. In writing for brass, I would have a recognizable unison line that compliments what the other instruments are doing. Then, I would usually split the brass into harmony at the end of a phrase.

6. Memorize each song and where possible sing along during the service. You will play with more passion when you own a song. Try transposing your parts into other keys, without writing the notes down. This is great ear training.

7. When in doubt, don't play. Although there is space for you to fill, sometimes it is better left as space. Learn to enjoy these moments.

Singers

1. Be aware of your strengths and weaknesses. Work on your weaknesses and allow your strengths to shine when singing in the team. If you need a regular singing lesson then seek out the best possible teacher in your area.

2. Be very aware of your pitch, especially when singing with others. If you are having trouble holding a part then swap with another.

3. Learn your part and stick to it. When unison is called for sing unison. Be disciplined. Bring a tape recorder to each rehearsal so you can practice your parts at home.

4. Learn the words to each song. Do not read off the slides or lyric sheets on the floor. Be an example to the congregation in your manner of worship. Do not be afraid to enter into worship while on the platform.

5. Listen to the singers around you. If you can't hear everybody then perhaps you're too loud. Make every effort to blend with the other voices in the group. Be sensitive to quiet moments. Don't sing just because there is music behind you. Learn to enjoy space.

6. Make each song your own. Let the conviction of your soul convey every word sung. People should believe every word that comes out of your mouth.

7. Sing with the musicians, not against them. Don't rush or drag your phrasing. Be sensitive to creating a whole sound of music and worship that helps the congregation sing along with you.

Sound Engineers

1. Find out from the pastor or music director the theme and order of each service along with any special songs, announcements or readings. Make it your responsibility to know what is expected of you.

2. Assume that people will be late and technical problems will occur. The general rule of thumb is to hope for the best but plan for the worst.

3. No matter how complicated or simple your sound system is, work to a plan. Number each microphone and cable and try to keep inputs in the same order for each service. Name each channel on the board so at any time you can easily change a level or EQ setting.

4. Maintain all equipment and keep a log book of any repairs. Prepare a yearly budget for maintenance and improvement and submit it to the music director.

5. Work with the musicians and singers to achieve the best possible sound. Help the

musicians find solutions to their volume problems. If instruments don't need to go through the system, then do not mic them. Keep the volume to a pleasant minimum—people need to be able hear themselves sing and think.

6. Insist on a sound check before each service. How much time do you need? Be finished at least fifteen minutes before the service begins.

7. Educate yourself in the art of engineering. Attend workshops, clinics and seminars. If you are unsure about anything, please ask someone who knows. I would highly recommend the book *A Guide to Sound Systems for Worship* by Jon F. Eiche (published by Hal Leonard). Each sound engineer should have a copy. It would be a very good investment for your church.

These are not exhaustive job descriptions. They do however, provide a foundation for a team work mentality amongst the people. Before each service, I would verbalize many of these directions to encourage everyone to make music together. Then I would insist on a time of corporate prayer and worship before any notes are played. When we truly humble ourselves together in prayer, the making of music becomes a much simpler task.

Chapter 10

What Do I Do Now?

"The important thing is to do,
and nothing else; be what it may."
Picasso

"Don't learn the tricks of the trade,
learn the trade."
Anonymous

The position of worship leader or music director is intended for someone with a flair for creativity. However, much of the work relates to the management of both time and people, and while we may hate the feeling of being boxed in or fenced off, we are more productive and effective when we have a basic plan to which we work.

During the first month of my employment,

a basic job description was handed to me by the assistant pastor and it evolved over the years to be something like this:

1. Pray and seek God every day

It really makes no difference whether you are full-time, part time or a volunteer minister; it is essential to pray and seek God every day. Praying, studying the Word and waiting on God takes discipline and effort. Often full-time ministers get so busy doing the things of God, they can forget about the precious quiet moments alone with God.

Pastor Phil Pringle was a good role model for me. I would often see him praying at the back of the sanctuary during office hours. I know that he was on his knees most mornings before sun up and would often walk and pray at night around the local golf course—probably claiming it as his own.

I remember one day when I desperately needed to speak with him but was told by his secretary that his schedule for the day was full.

Early that afternoon I saw Pastor Phil sitting by himself in the church and I thought to myself, "Huh. . . too busy eh?!" I hurried over with my very important question only to find him lost in prayer. I crept away quietly before I disturbed him and felt both ashamed for my attitude and impressed with his discipline to schedule his day with a time of prayer.

The best leaders lead by example. If you can build and manage a life of prayer you will raise up like-minded people around you.

Usually I like to sing and pray. It is easier for me to pray for long periods if I put it into a song. I know it sounds strange but that's what works for me. Other times I will walk and pray. The walking helps me to stay focused. I'll walk either back and forth in a room or out in the streets. Street prayer walking is best at night after dinner or early in the morning when there is no one about.

For worshipping the Lord, I presently have several places to which I disappear. One is the dining room (converted into an office) and the other is the garage. They both function as quiet places for me where I can sing or just strum unto the Lord.

I would encourage you to find your own

quiet place where you can seek out and find the Lord for yourself. Learning to wait in His presence takes time, patience and discipline but the rewards are out of this world.

2. Prepare music for church services

After a meeting with the pastoral team to discuss the theme and direction of the services, it would be my responsibility to shape the music and worship.

This would mean co-ordinating musicians, singers and sound engineers for the services, organizing either a mid week or (very) early pre-service rehearsal, writing charts for any new songs and making sure there was music and slides for anything we might possibly sing.

For those of you who don't read or write music, you will need to find an assistant who can help you to write out the music or help you to explain your arrangements to the musicians and singers.

The responsibility for choosing songs was shared week to week. Sometimes the pastor had definite thoughts on how the worship would flow and other weeks he would leave it up to whoever was leading worship.

The greatest preparation we can do is to pray and ask God for wisdom. He has a plan for each service and, if we are open to it, we will flow with Him and His Spirit.

There are times when I'll feel an urgency to include a certain song and even though I don't always know why, it's all part of learning to flow in the Spirit. Sometimes I will feel vindicated because the pastor preached from the same text as the song was written or perhaps someone will tell me after the service how God had touched them through that song.

In any event, it is important to stay open. There have also been times when I have not followed my instincts and have felt a like fool for letting the congregation down.

Writing everything down is another good discipline. If my pastor gave me some instructions, I wrote it in my organizer. As I began to develop the song list I would jot down any ideas I had on the arrangements. Once the arrangements were clear in my mind, I would sketch them out in musical form. Rehearsals were more time efficient if I had a plan written for others to follow.

Good preparation also allows us to be more flexible. The one thing that is certain in life is that things will change so be prepared for it to take place.

3. Train musicians, singers and sound engineers

I began with a team of about thirty people which grew steadily into a team of over a hundred, so the training worked best by dividing people into the three different groups for weekly practical training sessions. Then a monthly meeting was scheduled where we would all come together for a quality time of worship. We never put a time limit on the worship and it was often deeper and sweeter than the worship during the actual church services.

Although the singers and sound engineers were officially under my care, I appointed people with skill and confidence to give more attention to each group.

The singers would meet on a midweek

evening at the church to work out parts and arrangements for any new songs as well as rehearse any songs that needed extra work.

The sound engineers would meet at either the leader's house or the church on Tuesday evenings to carry out post mortems on the previous week's meetings and discuss how to fix any problems. I would visit these meetings periodically to encourage and to offer suggestions for improvement. However, the leaders were fully able to raise up and train others on their own.

The musicians were looked after by myself or another experienced musician. Because of everybody's busy schedules, we chose to rehearse before each service. This would mean a very early 6.30 A.M. start on Sunday mornings and a 4 P.M. start on Sunday afternoon in preparation for the evening service. If there was too much to learn, we would get together on a Saturday afternoon with some of the singers and sound engineers as well.

I have never been one for over rehearsing as this easily drains the life out of songs and musicians. There needs to be a good balance between rehearsing and jamming. Often the best ideas come from just having fun together.

4. Train leaders

By this I mean train other worship leaders, band leaders, songwriters, leaders of the sound engineers and singers, and people with the potential to carry leadership roles in the future.

In the beginning, I found this to be the most difficult of all my duties. I was at fault many times for communicating my desires poorly, especially to those closest to me.

At the suggestion of my pastor, I started a twice monthly small group meeting in my home. Inviting key people (and their spouses), we worshipped, prayed and fellowshipped together, often into the early hours of the morning.

This was when deep friendships were formed and many relationship problems were healed over coffee, pastries and my wife's famous cheese platter. Out of this small group, songs, albums, careers and ministries were birthed. All of these people are succeeding today in their chosen professions. Some are involved in full-time ministry and some manage their own businesses while others are working for television stations and large recording companies around the world.

I learned that good fellowship is even more important to a team's well being than any training or rehearsal.

5. Organize music for special events

This would mean finding songs to compliment the theme or occasion and finding singers (either from within or outside the congregation) to perform them. It would also mean writing music charts, rehearsing with the musicians and singers, drawing up stage plans for the lighting and sound engineers, and with an outside event, overseeing the production.

Some of these events were very draining for my family, my team and me, so I had to carefully plan the rehearsals to prevent people from burning out. The more organized and prepared I was for each rehearsal, the more we were able to achieve in the shortest amount of time. Good pre-production is the key to success for all major events.

I learned to share quite a number of these

responsibilities with others and with that came an increase in both productivity and creativity. The sharing of success is important; however when things don't go as well as they had been planned, a leader must accept that account on his or her own.

6. Find or write new songs

Finding new songs meant listening to new worship albums or traveling to other churches to hear what new songs they were singing. This was and continues to be a very subjective task. What sounds good on a tape may or may not work in a congregational setting. What helps one congregation sing unto the Lord may hinder another.

It is very important to know the style of music and language with which your congregation feels most comfortable. Many times a song I thought would work plummeted without a parachute, while a song I did not particularly like was accepted and enjoyed by the congregation for many years.

Sometimes an old song with a new arrangement serves better than teaching another new song on the same subject. But then sometimes a new song introduced in the right season will quickly become an anthem to the church. Who can tell?

It would also be my responsibility to gain copyright permission and make slides for the overhead projectors, although I delegated these tasks to another willing soul as soon as possible.

Our church was blessed with some great writers of worship songs so a great deal of our worship material each weekend was written specifically for our congregation. It didn't take long for me to be caught up in this wave of creative ministry. Over the years, I have worked hard at developing the craft of songwriting and would now consider myself as much a songwriter as a worship leader.

7. Facilitate music for small groups

As the cell or small home group was an integral part of our church, there was a great need for sheet music of the songs we used on a Sunday.

To help the average musician lead worship, I would write simple chord charts with typed lyrics, choosing keys that worked well on both piano and guitar. For many songs, I had to find alternative chords as most of these musicians were not familiar with an A minor half-diminished chord.

This was not an easily solved problem as people would complain that the song wasn't as musically recognizable with the simple chords. To solve this, we held classes to teach theory and harmony for both guitar and piano.

After a while, we became more organized and produced song books and sheet music in true published form. We thought it important to also include an explanation of why we wrote each song as well as include suggestions for the arrangement and use of the songs.

8. Musically preside over weddings and funerals

For each wedding ceremony I had to supply music, musicians and special songs. On average there were about twenty weddings per year and on some weekends, more than one.

On one particular Saturday we participated in three consecutive wedding ceremonies. During the third wedding the pastor, a little flustered and tired, completely forgot the names of the bride and groom and gave each of them a name from one of the previous two weddings. The musicians were the only ones who laughed.

Funerals would require one or two musicians and maybe some singers. It was important to provide the grieving family with music and songs of their choice. The most difficult job was finding musicians who wanted to play at a funeral.

9. Harness the gifts of others

Without the help of other people, I would have never been able to accomplish all the tasks of a worship leader and keep my sanity. This is fitting as leading worship was never meant to be a one person show. Learning to delegate tasks to a person who would take ownership of even a simple duty like phoning people for rehearsals was a skill that I developed over time.

The hardest thing about delegation was giving up things that I liked to do. However, as the team grew, it was important to let people shine in their strengths.

Writing and arranging music was something I had done for a living and for the first year or so that duty was left to me alone. It was not long, however, before other fine musicians were writing and arranging for the services. I had to train myself to let go of some of the things I liked to do and teach myself to enjoy the contribution of their gifts.

Delegation and management were not skills that came naturally to me. I was aided by several friends who guided me in the developing of others. Whereas I knew what I liked to hear from singers and could teach vocal parts, I was not able to improve their vocal technique. God provided someone with years of vocal training experience to fill this ministry.

The sound system needed updating and the sound engineers needed training but as neither of these were in my field of expertise, God provided an experienced sound engineer to take the lead role.

One of the greatest mandates of a leader is to be perceptive to the gifted people God is sending you. So often God can be supplying the people that the ministry needs but our noses are so close to the 'grinding wheel' that we do not recognize that they are standing there waiting to be asked.

I would learn over time to accept wisdom and advice from many people with more experience than me. Accommodating their gifts and expertise greatly multiplied the effectiveness of what I was doing. Whatever my plans and visions for my team, they were significantly enhanced by the input of my leaders and team members.

Planted by the Water

My mind goes back to the day when my predecessor threw me the keys to my new office and wished me luck. I did not realize it then, but that was the beginning of a great adventure that continues to excite me today.

It may have been my child-like faith and naivete that cried out 'Okay, I'll try something new', but it has been the grace, mercy and patience of the Father that carried me over the mountains, through the deserts and across the troubled waters.

So often I have imagined myself as the tree planted by the water as referred to in Jeremiah 17. Had I not learned to be still before the Lord and draw upon His refreshing water, I would have withered under the sun's intensity and bearing fruit would have been impossible.

Like a tree, my instincts must be to draw upon His nourishment every day. For I realize that it is not the success of my plans that sustains me, but the presence of the Lord. He is the provider of growth in all aspects of my life and ministry.

I will always encourage musicians and

singers who are serious about developing their skill to submit to the discipline of college or private tuition. This is good stewardship of the talents God has given us.

However, when it comes to turning hearts towards Christ, all the skill in the world is no substitute for His anointing. The sensitivity to the Spirit of God and the anointing to lead people in worship can only be received by having spent time in the Lord's presence. Practice and tuition is important. But time with the Lord, the master teacher Himself, is essential.

I believe the Church is entering a new chapter in history. God is searching for worshippers who will worship Him in spirit and in truth, and who will do so without the fear of man. Many of these worshippers will raise up armies of like-minded, free spirited people who will seek the Lord day and night.

As a fresh wave of creative freedom flows through the body of Christ many musicians, singers and artists will take this freedom out into the marketplace for the world to taste the Lord's goodness and mercy.

The Lord is calling: "Who will go in my name?"

No matter how inadequate I may feel for the challenge ahead, I know where my strength comes from and my prayer remains: "Here am I Lord, please use me."

About the Author

Chris Falson has recorded several solo albums and travels extensively in his ministry of leading and teaching worship. Many of his songs have been recorded by artists around the world. Chris lives in Los Angeles with his wife and their two sons.

Chris Falson Products

A Tree by the Water
More of Jesus
Peace of God
Holy Spirit
The Throne Room
and more. . .

***For Dreamers Only
(Instrumental)***
Peaceful contemplative music

Live Worship
Chris Falson & The Amazing Stories
Let Me Be a Worshipper
I See the Lord
Pure Joy
All Honor ***and more. . .***

Chris Falson (Self Titled)
Can You Go the Distance
Jamming with the Angels
Cool Water
One Day
and more. . .

Produced by Chris Falson for Maranatha! Music
Featuring various artists and writers

***Standing
on the
Rock***

Pure Joy

Song from Heaven
For the Rest of My Days
Come Holy Spirit
and more. . .

I Delight in the Lord
Holy & Righteous
All Things
Pure Joy ***and more. . .***

To order other Chris Falson products:

Visit website: **www.chrisfalson.com**

OR

Call or fax 1-626-403-5780
(Toll free 1-888-257-5788 in USA only)

OR

Write to: The Orchard
P.O. Box 80008
San Marino CA 91118
USA